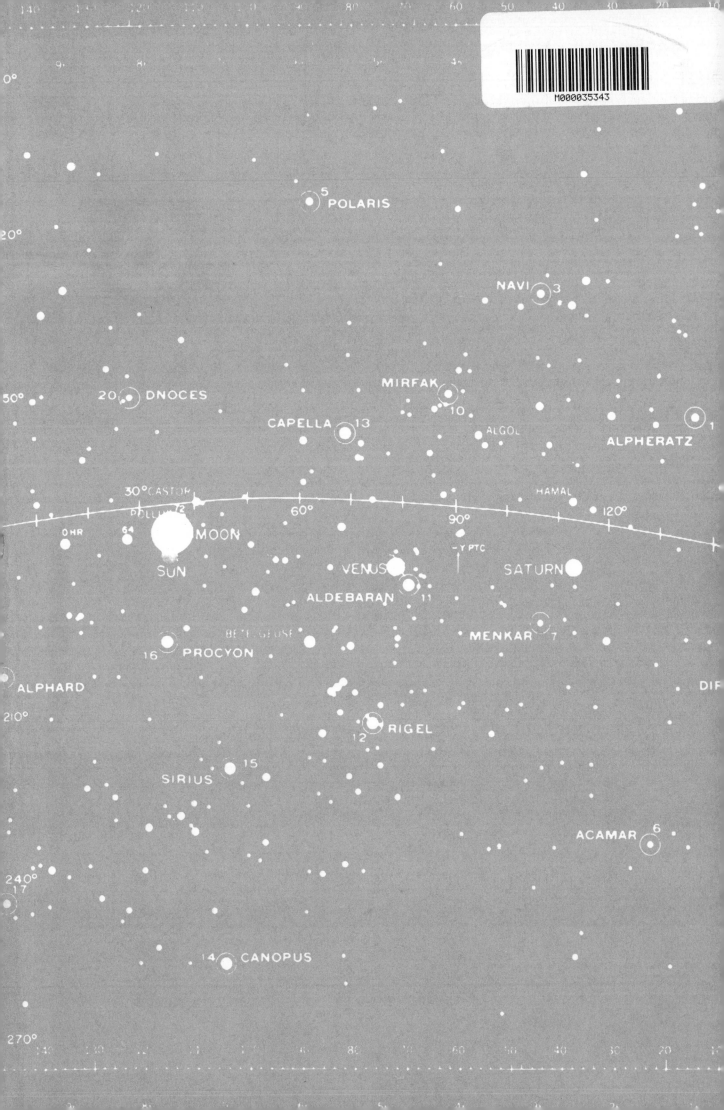

# ARTIFACTS OF FLIGHT

CAROLYN RUSSO
FOREWORD BY JOHN GLENN
INTRODUCTION BY TED A. MAXWELL

SMITHSONIAN NATIONAL AIR AND SPACE MUSEUM, WASHINGTON, D.C.
IN ASSOCIATION WITH HARRY N. ABRAMS, INC., PUBLISHERS

Special thanks to Pratt & Whitney for its generous support.

In-kind donations from Ilford Imaging USA, Inc.

Editor: Richard Slovak
Designer: Binocular, New York
Production Manager: Jane Searle

Library of Congress Cataloging-in-Publication Data
Russo, Carolyn.
 Artifacts of flight / Carolyn Russo; foreword by John Glenn; introduction by Ted A. Maxwell.
    p.   cm.
Includes index.
  ISBN 0-8109-4530-4
 1. National Air and Space Museum--Catalogs. 2. Aeronautics--United States--History--Pictorial works. 3. Astronautics--United States--History--Pictorial works.
I. National Air and Space Museum.
II. Title.
  TL506.U6.W3767 2003
  629.1'074'09753--dc21
            2003005346

Printed and bound in Italy
10 9 8 7 6 5 4 3 2 1

Harry N. Abrams, Inc.
100 Fifth Avenue
New York, N.Y. 10011
www.abramsbooks.com

Abrams is a subsidiary of:

LA MARTINIÈRE
G R O U P E

Previous spread: Detail of the afterburner section of a Pratt & Whitney J-58 Ramjet engine on the SR-71 reconnaissance aircraft (see pages 136–37).

This spread: The landing gear, wing root, and shock cone of the SR-71.

Overleaf: The Ansco Autoset/ Minolta Hi-Matic Camera used by astronaut John Glenn during his historic orbital space flight in 1962.

Page 8: The door of the *Spirit of St. Louis*; the skin of the airplane was originally fashioned from

Flightex fabric made with Arizona Pima cotton — but repaired with a French cotton material after souvenir hunters mobbed the plane in Paris (see page 54).

Page 160: The aft fuselage of *Enterprise* (OV-101), the first full-scale Space Shuttle orbiter (see page 40).

Endpapers: Star chart used by command-module pilot Michael Collins during the Apollo 11 mission to the Moon (see page 53).

For Bob and Max

Every day hundreds of simple drugstore cameras can be found inside the Smithsonian's National Air and Space Museum. Only one stays past closing time. I bought it in January 1962 after a haircut in Cocoa Beach, Florida. By then my attempt to be the first American in orbit had been delayed several times, giving me more opportunity to press NASA to let me take pictures during the flight. Al Shepard's and Gus Grissom's suborbital missions the previous year had lasted only about fifteen minutes each, too short for snapshots. I wanted to give people an idea of what astronauts saw outside their spacecraft so they could better relate to our often highly technical endeavors. Satellite photography was already becoming commonplace, but I felt there was no substitute for human judgment controlling a lens and shutter.

I don't recall what the barber charged that day, but a visit with the druggist next door turned up a forty-five-dollar Ansco Autoset/Minolta Hi-Matic. I was immediately sold on the 35-mm camera's automatic exposure system, which meant I wouldn't have to tinker with light meters and f-stops through the thick gloves of my silver pressure suit. After NASA technicians added a pistol grip and oversized film advance, Mission Control was convinced photography wouldn't distract me from the flight checklist and safety. More expensive cameras were tested, but nothing matched the ease of that drugstore point-and-shoot.

On February 20, 1962, I made three orbits of Earth and thirty-eight photographs with the Hi-Matic. Most memorable were images of clouds over the Canaries and massive dust storms in the Sahara Desert. Still, it is possible some good shots got away as I flew 17,500 miles an hour. While changing film at one point, I accidentally knocked the new roll behind the instrument panel. I waited a moment for it to fall back into view, only to realize it wouldn't in the zero gravity of space.

\* \* \*

Missing a great photograph can be a risk of visiting the National Air and Space Museum on the Mall in Washington. There are three blocks' worth of galleries to wander, and artifacts like my Ansco/Minolta must be kept behind glass in dim lighting. Then there are those treasures, often too large or too fragile, that must be stored away.

With this book, museum photographer Carolyn Russo puts the unequaled scope of the national collection in our hands, presenting both the icons and the unfamiliar in stark, eloquent composition. Even my crushed tube of 1962 applesauce — the first American meal in space — makes an appearance, another silent witness to a century of progress in powered flight, complete with bits of Velcro still attached.

Over the years I've been photographed by Carolyn Russo dozens of times. When she's creating the shot, she's firmly in charge no matter what the subject may be. As you can see from the images that follow, her unyielding photographic judgment brings new life to the relics of flight and the achievements they represent.

This book of Air and Space treasures is a treasure in itself.

007-

# foreword by john glenn

John Glenn was the first American astronaut to orbit Earth

Fifty-nine seconds is not a lot of time. As you read this, the Pioneer 10 spacecraft, launched in 1972, will travel 448 miles in fifty-nine seconds. A Boeing 747 will travel about seven and a half miles. Yet on December 17, 1903, the Wright Flyer, powered by a 12-horsepower engine, made its longest flight of 852 feet in fifty-nine seconds. A hundred years later, we now realize what those first few seconds of flight engendered: world travel measured in hours instead of weeks, commercial airline travel faster than the speed of sound, the ability to map the surface of Earth from vantage points of a few hundred feet to a thousand miles, ingenious methods to spy on people and countries, and much more. These achievements, some dreamed of and some never imagined, are woven so tightly into our experience that we can lose sight of how momentous each step in their direction seemed when it was taken. Through artifacts like the ones collected in this book, we can begin to understand and appreciate how each new breakthrough in manned flight expanded the horizons of the people who witnessed them. You may know that the Wright brothers ran a bicycle shop, but it is not until you see the bicycle sprocket on the front of the 1903 Wright Flyer that you can really appreciate the technology they had to work with.

We live in a world of gear — camping gear, sports gear, cold-weather gear, even L.A. Gear, fills our closets. It wasn't until the advent of cabin pressurization in the late 1940s, however, that humans could travel long distances in aircraft without special gear to ensure their health and comfort. At the museum, gear clutters our storerooms. Wiley Post, for example, was able to soar to a record-breaking 40,000 feet in his Lockheed Vega in 1934 thanks only to a pressure suit of his own devising, based on deep-sea suits and designed to provide similar environmental support, and we've got it. I found myself thinking about Post recently on a commercial flight where the in-flight monitor kept reminding me that the outside temperature was –37 degrees Fahrenheit. The sheepskin-lined hats and gloves, flying goggles, and scarves required by fliers well into the twentieth century seem quaint today, when our climate control consists of reaching up from the seat and twisting a little air vent. In the space business, gear is still the way to go: it's called "life-support systems." A lot of this gear, unlike the gear of early aviators, is still in use — the Space Shuttle astronauts are using recycled equipment, refurbished and resized from astronaut to astronaut. This makes it difficult to collect relics of current technology, and indeed, an entire company exists to provide replica spacesuits for museums and expositions. For space missions, the National Air and Space Museum often makes do with demonstrators and prototypes that never left Earth's atmosphere.

Why care about all of this stuff? Books abound on the history of flight, those who made it happen, and the aircraft and spacecraft that were the technological triumphs of their day. What is the purpose of the National Collection of Aviation and Space Artifacts? It is more than collecting the air- and spacecraft that fill the halls of the museum. It is to preserve treasures that tell us about people, with needs like ours for basic warmth and comfort, who in the midst of extraordinary achievements scribbled notes on the dashboard or the back of a piece of paper just as we do. To remind us that the practical objects that make manned flight possible also possess beauty and individuality, from

# introduction by ted a. maxwell

Ted A. Maxwell is Associate
Director, Collections and Research,
Smithsonian Institution
National Air and Space Museum

the lightweight wicker seat that Charles Lindbergh installed in the *Spirit of St. Louis* to the Valsalva device inside the space helmets of astronauts that these resourceful characters use to scratch their noses. To evoke the spirit of the air, seen for example in the understated humor that has become the hallmark of "pilot-speak," as manifested in such things as a "towing invoice" for the dramatic safe return of Apollo 13. To document through ordinary objects like song sheets and lunchboxes the constant presence of manned flight in our daily lives.

And, of course, to serve as a repository of primary information for the historian of flight. The Smithsonian made a special effort to collect significant objects related to the pioneers of flight, but was not always tactful in its efforts. In 1899 Wilbur Wright wrote to Secretary Langley of the Smithsonian requesting his assistance in gathering scientific information on flight. Samuel P. Langley, the third Secretary of the Institution, had published papers on his own experiments in aerodynamics and at the time had a War Department grant to build a manned airplane. The Smithsonian replied, sending Wilbur published papers and references to other works. However, when Orville Wright later considered donating their 1903 Wright Flyer to the Institution, he found in the Smithsonian an exhibit label stating that Langley's Aerodrome A was the first airplane *capable* of sustained free flight. Nonplussed, he loaned the Flyer to the Museum of Science in London, where it remained until 1948. Eventually, it was curator Paul Garber who helped make possible the return of the aircraft. To put the earlier misunderstanding to rest, the Smithsonian agreed to the wording in the contract stating, "Neither the Smithsonian Institution or its successors nor any museum or other agency, bureau or facilities, administered for the United States of America by the Smithsonian Institution . . . shall publish or permit to be dis-

played a statement or label in connection with or in respect of any aircraft model or design of earlier date than the Wright Aeroplane of 1903, claiming in effect that such aircraft was capable of carrying a man under its own power in controlled flight." Eventually, numerous artifacts — some reproduced in this book — related to the first powered manned flight entered the collection.

Secretary Langley, by the way, was interested in both air and space. He had developed several unmanned aircraft with the help of funding from the Army and flew them off of a houseboat moored in the Potomac — no doubt for political visibility as much as for tests of their mechanics. The Aerodrome was his final bid for first flight, but when it crashed on launch in the fall of 1903, he gave up his experiments in aviation to concentrate on his scientific observations of the sun, for which he is still well known.

The years between World Wars I and II are remembered as the Golden Age of Flight. As in any golden age, its heroes were immensely famous in their day and are legends to us now — none more so than the resplendent Charles Lindbergh and the tragic Amelia Earhart. The event that catapulted Lindbergh into history is well known. Earhart's was a disappearing act. On July 2, 1937, she took off with Fred Noonan, her navigator and copilot, on the last leg of an around-the-world flight. They were never heard from again. Every so often a letter or phone call to the museum asks us if we have the airplane in which she disappeared. Despite numerous searches, the most recent with side-scanning sonar, no trace has yet been found. The museum, of course, possesses many artifacts related to these two pilots, some pictured in this book.

In the Golden Age, fliers vied for world's records, some to prove a point to financiers, others simply because a record existed to be broken — and broken they were, with amazing frequency and leaps of time and distance. The *Vin Fiz*, a Wright airplane named after a soft drink, had taken forty-nine days to fly across the United States in 1911. In 1924, two Douglas World Cruisers circled the entire globe in six months. Just nine years later, Wiley Post made the same trip solo in less than eight days. The Schneider, Bendix, and Thompson Trophies; the Orteig Prize; the Hearst Award — these now-legendary grails, and many others, all combined to accelerate technological change.

Eyes were trained well beyond the atmosphere in the 1920s and 1930s. In the Soviet Union, Konstantin Tsiolkovsky, who published *The Exploration of Space with Reaction Propelled Devices* the same year as the Wrights' epic flight, was the inspiration for generations of rocket experimenters. In Germany, the Verein für Raumschiffahrt (Society for Space Travel), boasting such notable members as Wernher von Braun, Hermann Oberth, and Johannes Winkler, was well established by 1930. The American Interplanetary Society, founded that year, initially consisted of a mix of science-fiction writers and serious experimentalists, who later separated into their respective fields. It is interesting to note that the science fiction of Jules Verne and Tsiolkovsky (who had feet in both camps), which inspired the pre–World War II generation of rocket scientists, was later disavowed by their successors who pushed the envelope. Even the Guggenheim Aeronautical Laboratory of Caltech shunned the word "rocket" in naming the Jet Propulsion Laboratory in 1943. Buck Rogers and Flash Gordon didn't have to worry about the stigma of naming, nor did they face the technical challenges of creating a liquid-filled rocket capable of propelling a payload out of Earth's gravity.

The Smithsonian was involved from the beginning with American pioneers of rocketry. As early as 1919, the Smithsonian Miscellaneous Collections Series included a monograph entitled *A Method of Reaching Extreme Altitudes*, with visions of spaceflight, by a young physicist named Robert H. Goddard.

The Collections Series was the appropriate venue for his results, which had been financially supported by the Institution. In 1926, Goddard successfully launched the world's first liquid-fueled rocket. Historically significant rockets, by nature perishable, are rare in museum collections — the Smithsonian is lucky to have one of Goddard's A-Series rockets, donated in 1935.

While the science fiction published in magazines like *Amazing Stories* made space travel seem easy and good guys invincible, the rocket scientists of Germany came under the influence of the Nazi Party, an evil empire that proved more difficult to dislodge than the villains of the pulps. World War II led not only to such technical advances as massive bombers and strategic bombing, maneuverable fighters, navigation systems, radar, jet engines, surveillance technology, pressurized cabins, aircraft carrier–capable planes, and a host of other accomplishments; it also gave the United States an entire new class of heroes. Within five months of the attack on Pearl Harbor, James Doolittle led sixteen B-25s in an attack on Tokyo. The pilots and crews knew they couldn't return to the aircraft carrier *Hornet*, since the runway was not long enough, and they were loaded with only enough fuel to fly over Japan and hopefully reach nearby China or Russia. Fifteen of the planes crashed after the attack — only one landed safely. Jackie Cochran, the indomitable winner of speed, altitude, and long-distance records, spent the war years ferrying aircraft from the United States to Britain and organizing the Women Airforce Service Pilots. The tough Curtis LeMay championed low-level night bombing of Japan, hastening the end of the war. These, and many other notable achievers — often anonymous — of the World War II era are represented in the museum's collection by aircraft and personal belongings that bring them to life.

After the war, civilian and military progress in aviation kept pace. With the development of the operational jet engine concurrently by Frank Whittle in Great Britain and Hans Von Ohain in Germany, both fighter and passenger aircraft could fly higher and more efficiently than ever before. While airplanes grew in complexity, the role of daring pilots seemed to diminish. It is interesting to note that Chuck Yeager broke the sound barrier in 1947, before the first half century of powered flight had come to an end. As throughout the history of aviation, technological advances in one aspect of aircraft construction exposed weaknesses in others — it took a series of crashes of the De Havilland Comet, the first British jetliner, to acquaint engineers with the problem of metal fatigue. And as always, tragic losses led to improvements in design and construction: by 1958, the Boeing 707, the forerunner of today's passenger jet, was born. With the appeal of commercial aviation came other kinds of appeals — even sex appeal. Airlines offering a service that was suddenly affordable to the middle classes began vying with one another for customers. Some lured passengers via short skirts and attractive stewardesses; others promoted images based on national customs or brash futurism. The museum has more than a few costumes in its closets to prove it, as the reader of this book will discover. Now, as we consider the possibility that we will have to *buy* airline food for our next flight, we may want to emulate Lindbergh in 1927: bring a few sandwiches and a canteen of water.

Other than food (which surprisingly enough also features prominently in the collection), there are few things we have to worry about as passengers on a commercial jet. Luckily, we don't have to equip ourselves with pressure suits that counteract g forces through tight maneuvers, or with ejection seats that can launch us to 100 miles per hour in less than half a second. Not so with military pilots of the last fifty years. The ability of jet engines to propel aircraft to supersonic speeds, of thrust nozzles spaced strategically on planes to force tight turns, and of the pilots themselves, always pushing the limits of their aircraft, combined to produce a different kind of tactical combat. Instead of the traditional "dogfight" that had been the hallmark of air-to-air combat since World War I, today's airborne missiles can target planes miles away, creating the need for stealth technologies. Air-to-ground missiles can wreak such specific havoc that they have largely replaced the need for indiscriminate bombs carried on huge aircraft.

Cold War arsenals of strategic bombers, ICBMs, and fighter aircraft, heralding devastating destruction, led to the development of more sophisticated weapons in the war of intelligence. The Lockheed U-2, the first operational stratospheric spy plane, was used to great advantage by the United States in the 1950s and 1960s. It is perhaps best remembered for the political uproar caused when Francis Gary Powers was shot down over Russia in 1960, but more importantly, it was a U-2 that confirmed the presence of missiles in Cuba in 1962, making it impossible for the Soviets to deny that they had armed that island nation. Along with spy satellites such as Corona in 1960 and follow-on spacecraft, the U-2 and its replacement, the SR-71 Blackbird, provided real-time intelligence to the United States.

While Powers was imprisoned in Russia (and writing the diary that is reproduced in this book), a new variant on the Cold War was announced by President John F. Kennedy. He charged the nation to put a man on the Moon within the decade. Supported by funding voted by a willing Congress, NASA achieved this national goal on July 20, 1969. The voyage of Neil Armstrong, Michael Collins, and Buzz Aldrin was not without its own martyrs: Ed White, Gus Grissom, and Roger Chaffee died in a fire in an Apollo capsule two years before the successful landing. They can be seen on a poster promoting safety, printed shortly before the accident, that someone thoughtfully donated to the collection. With the exception of spacesuits, lunar-sample boxes, and the modules themselves, few of the objects that landed on the Moon returned. We've established the first museum storage facility on the Moon: three lunar rovers, along with everything from the lunar-module descent engines to rock hammers and rakes, remain there awaiting the attention of some eager curator of the future. The process of collecting these artifacts of lunar exploration actually began on the Apollo 12 mission. In 1969, astronauts retrieved a camera from the Surveyor 3 unmanned spacecraft and brought it back to Earth after its two-year stay on the Moon. It eventually ended up in the National Air and Space Museum, minus a few small pieces cut out to study the longevity of items left in the lunar environment. Even now, serious planning to fly an unpiloted airplane over Mars, with a variety of cameras and sensors, has begun. Perhaps Mars is destined to be the back lot of a future airport.

No matter what our science-fiction writers have told us, the difficulties of putting a human being in an artificial environment subjected to the pulls of gravity (or no gravity), and keeping him or her supplied with air, food, and water, have proved to be daunting. It took 363 feet of a three-stage Saturn 5 to launch just three men to the Moon, and, even now, it requires two solid rocket boosters and a huge external fuel tank to launch the Space Shuttle into low Earth orbit. To venture beyond the Earth-Moon system will require more life support than we have yet mastered — one of the prime purposes of the International Space Station is to begin to learn just how much more. The problems of muscle degeneration and bone loss resulting from extended periods in reduced gravity will require years of research on long-duration missions, to be matched only by the engineering challenges of developing a low-cost, secure means of venturing into space. The losses of the Space Shuttles *Challenger* and *Columbia* remind us that we are still at the beginning of spaceflight, and, as in the early days of flight in the atmosphere, we will learn much from each of our mistakes. Meanwhile, there are artifacts aplenty in this book to remind us of the joys and the terrors of manned spaceflight so far.

There remain, of course, many items of interest in the collection that never made it to these pages. The common flush rivet — an important innovation in metal aircraft construction — is missing here, and so is the space toilet (the collection contains both U.S. and Russian models), a necessary device that is more complicated than you would think, given the conditions of microgravity in which it must function. With more than 45,000 objects individually accounted for, the collection grows and shrinks each month. What were acquisitioned as collections from individuals and corporations half a century ago are now being catalogued as individual items. Meanwhile, flight instruments once catalogued individually are now being relocated to restored aircraft and spacecraft, reducing this collection one by one, but adding completeness to another.

The National Air and Space Museum does not have a stranglehold on aviation memorabilia; the collection cannot possibly house all that either our curators or aerospace experts think we should have. We take seriously our charge to care for and memorialize the treasures of aviation and space, and consider carefully all that is offered to us. But we are not alone in this endeavor. Aviation and space museums are located in every part of the country, and each contains a perspective special to its region or subject. Each one has some of the real stuff that reminds us of the people who have made aviation and spaceflight possible.

**WRIGHT BROTHERS' STOPWATCH**
The Wright brothers tossed a coin to decide who would take the controls of their newest flying machine at Kitty Hawk, North Carolina, on December 14, 1903. With Wilbur in the pilot's position, the Wright Flyer rose momentarily into the air before it stalled, hitting the ground and sustaining some damage. Three days later, on December 17, they were ready for another attempt, this time with Orville at the controls.

Filled with confidence in the aircraft, Wilbur stood by with this nickel-plated stopwatch, purchased in 1892, in hand. At 10:35 A.M., the plane was launched from its rail and traveled 120 feet though the air in about twelve seconds. Wilbur was so amazed that he forgot to time the flight. They succeeded three more times that day, documenting the later results. Wilbur was at the controls for the best effort, traveling 852 feet and timed at fifty-nine seconds. One could only imagine their feelings as the inventors and pilots of the world's first powered airplane.

**THE WRIGHT FLYER** Orville and Wilbur Wright constructed the Wright Flyer in the back room of their bicycle shop, located at 1127 West Third Street in Dayton, Ohio. The aircraft was designed to manage pitch, roll, and yaw, the fundamental requirement for any machine intended for flight. Control was achieved by movement of the wings, a technique called "wing warping," which the brothers first tested through kite and glider flights. The Flyer's airframe was made of wood and covered with muslin. A homebuilt 4-cylinder, 12-horsepower engine powered two propellers via a sprocket-and-chain transmission system. After the Flyer was completed in sections, it was shipped down to Kitty Hawk, North Carolina, and assembled . . . and the world had its first successful powered heavier-than-air flying machine.

On the same day it completed the first historic flights, the Wright Flyer was swept up by a gust of wind and damaged beyond repair. It would never fly again. Over the next four decades, the Flyer was stored and exhibited in a variety of places. For the first ten years, it remained in a shed behind the Wrights' bicycle shop, where it suffered even more damage after being submerged in water and mud for almost two weeks during a flood in 1913. The craft traveled to England before making its way into the Smithsonian Institution in 1948. It hangs from the museum's ceiling at approximately the same height above the ground as its first flight, on December 17, 1903.

**HARRISON SCHMITT'S BOOTS** The last trip to the Moon was Apollo 17, launched on December 7, 1972, with Gene Cernan, Ron Evans, and Harrison Schmitt on board. Schmitt, the only geologist to walk on the Moon, was selected for the Scientist Astronaut program in 1965. He helped organize training for lunar astronauts and was the lead scientist in support of Apollo 11. He was also involved in the development of lunar hardware, and he supervised the final preparations of the Apollo lunar-module descent stage. After his training as backup lunar-module pilot for Apollo 15, he was the lunar-module pilot for Apollo 17.

On December 11, 1972, Schmitt and Cernan landed in the Valley of Taurus-Littrow on the southeastern edge of the Sea of Serenity. Thanks to Schmitt's extensive background as a lunar geologist, he naturally had a good understanding of Taurus-Littrow's features. Together they traveled the greatest distance over the lunar terrain in a lunar rover and, "like kids in a candy shop," collected the largest sampling of lunar rocks and soil of any Apollo mission. The specimens included various soils, lava, and crustal materials, weighing a total of more than 243 pounds. Schmitt and Cernan's final act was to leave a plaque on the lunar surface. It reads, "Here man completed his first exploration of the Moon, December 1972 A.D. May the spirit of peace in which he came be reflected in the lives of all mankind."

These boots were worn by Harrison Schmitt on Apollo 17 and are soiled with lunar dust. They were made to go over the pressure boots of the suit. Astronauts on previous missions left their boots behind because of the extra weight they added to the lunar module. The Apollo 17 astronauts recognized the significance of their last steps and brought them back.

**HINDENBURG RELICS** The *Hindenburg* made her maiden transatlantic voyage from Frankfurt, Germany, to Lakehurst, New Jersey, on May 6, 1936. The world's largest airship was 803.8 feet long and 135.1 feet in diameter. Four Daimler Benz 16-cylinder diesel engines powered the massive ship. Each propeller had four nineteen-foot blades. During her first year of operation, the *Hindenburg* carried more than 1,300 passengers paying the princely price of four hundred dollars for a one-way ocean crossing, gaining popularity for its sophisticated interior decorations and comfortable accommodations. The airship's future in transatlantic travel looked promising.

She was a symbol of luxury in transatlantic air travel. The hydrogen-filled floating palace accommodated passengers with the finest amenities. The dining-salon waiters poured superb wines and served gourmet meals on place settings of blue-and-gold porcelain. Private cabins were equipped with sleeping berths and showers. Travelers could stand at the vessel's open windows and hear dogs barking below while cruising at eighty knots, five hundred feet above the ground.

On May 6, 1937, precisely one year after her maiden flight, as the *Hindenburg* arrived at Lakehurst, New Jersey, the ship suddenly exploded into a hellish inferno. As Michael Mooney described the scene in his book about the disaster, "In Friday's dawn except for a half-burnt swastika still showing on its dislocated tail, and the eerie, twisted skeleton of a beached whale, its aluminum rib cage still glowing, there was nothing left." Theories regarding the cause ranged from ball lightning to burning hydrogen, and some even suspected sabotage. A more recent theory suggests that the doping solution used on the outer fabric of the airship consisted of a highly combustible material that could have been ignited by static electricity from the ground as she was mooring. Personnel at the Naval Air Station immediately made calls to local rescue workers, ambulance drivers, and doctors for assistance. Of the ninety-seven persons on board, sixty-two managed to escape from the inferno.

Jesse W. Lankford, chief of the Accident Analysis Section of the American Civil Aeronautics Board and an investigator of the accident, found this unbroken cup and saucer at the site of the catastrophe. A retired Navy chief, called to drive an ambulance, stepped on this propeller fragment; he picked it up and threw it under the driver's seat. Eventually these relics made their way into the museum's collection.

## ALAN SHEPARD'S SPACESUIT

Alan Shepard became the first American in space on May 5, 1961, when his *Freedom 7* spacecraft was launched atop an eighty-foot-tall, modified Redstone intermediate-range ballistic missile and he successfully piloted a fifteen-minute suborbital flight. It was a triumph for the American space program, but in comparison to Soviet cosmonaut Yuri Gagarin's one-and-three-quarter-hour orbital flight on April 12, 1961, it also demonstrated that his country had plenty of catching up to do.

The results of Shepard's flight provided NASA with baseline data for the future astronauts and spacecraft of the Mercury program. Shepard's physiological responses to the microgravity environment and the stresses of spaceflight — especially during launch and reentry — were monitored with instruments. The performance of the spacecraft was also recorded during all phases of the mission.

Mercury spacesuits, developed by the B.F. Goodrich Company, were customized versions of the Navy MK IV high-altitude suits worn in jet aircraft. They were pressurized in the event the spacecraft lost pressurization, but they could not have protected their wearers outside the spacecraft. The inner layer consisted of a Neoprene rubber-coated nylon fabric, and the outer layer was a heat-reflective silver aluminized nylon fabric. The silver exterior did indeed make the suits look futuristic.

Shepard experienced some problems with his suit during his flight. For example, it was reported that he had trouble reading his wrist gauge because his mobility was limited. After his flight, adjustments were made, including the addition of miniature lights on the index and middle fingers of the gloves to illuminate gauges on the instrument panel and charts.

### JOHN GLENN'S APPLESAUCE

John Glenn was the first American astronaut to orbit Earth, while piloting his *Friendship 7* spacecraft on February 20, 1962. Since the planned flight would be longer than any other attempted thus far, NASA scientists used the mission to experiment with food consumption. At the time, it was still unknown if food could be chewed, swallowed, and digested in zero gravity.

Mercury space foods were based on Army survival rations and consisted of pureed dishes packaged in aluminum tubes and ingested through a straw. They were designed to provide high-energy, nutritional meals with minimal preparation or eating time, but there was limited variety and they tasted awful. The snacks that were planned for Glenn's flight included applesauce and beef stew, as well as malted-milk balls. Glenn managed to pucker down half a tube of applesauce. One can only imagine why the beef stew remained untouched.

After a successful career as a U.S. senator, Glenn returned to space on October 29, 1998, thirty-six years later, joining a nine-day mission aboard the Space Shuttle *Discovery*. The seventy-nine-year-old crew member, and the oldest person so far to fly in space, was responsible for a variety of research payloads, including the deployment of the Spartan solar-observing spacecraft and the Hubble Space Telescope Orbital Systems Test Platform. Without a doubt, the food he experienced this time tasted much better.

The applesauce consumed by John Glenn during his *Friendship 7* flight was the first American meal eaten in space.

**EARLY PILOT LICENSES** In the early days of flying, rules and regulations regarding standards for pilots and their airplanes were incredibly lenient in comparison to nowadays. A flight certificate could be obtained from the Aero Club of America (later renamed the National Aeronautical Association, under the authority of Fédération Aéronautique Internationale) with minimal time in the cockpit and knowledge of regulations — because there weren't many. The U.S. military licensed civilian pilots during World War I, and some state governments issued certificates, but it was not until 1927 that the Aeronautics Branch of the Department of Commerce (now the Federal Aviation Administration, or FAA) issued federally regulated licenses.

The current regulations enforced on pilots and aircraft maintain a safer sky. To obtain a private pilot license from the FAA for a single-engine plane in VFR (Visible Flight Rules) conditions, you must be seventeen years of age; speak, understand, and read English; obtain a third-class medical certificate; receive ground-school instruction to learn air safety, regulations, and navigation; pass a written test; have a minimum of forty hours of flight time including twenty solo hours; and successfully complete a practical test given by an FAA flight examiner. The FAA issued 625,581 pilot certificates in the year 2000.

**CHARLES LINDBERGH'S PASSPORT PHOTO** In the late spring of 1927, a young man came into Isidore Culver's photographic studio at 29 Broadway in New York City requesting a passport photograph. He sat with his large hands resting across his lap, eyes staring intently, but not at the camera. As he got up to leave, he mentioned to the photographer that his name was Charles Lindbergh and that he was going to fly across the Atlantic Ocean — alone. Culver probably raised an eyebrow. The feat had never been accomplished, and often those who had tried experienced dreadful results.

A few weeks later, on May 20, the photographer read the news of Lindbergh's flight. Indeed, the passport had been a necessity after all. Realizing the importance of the event, Culver brought the glass-plate negative home for safekeeping. The negative remained in the family until Culver's granddaughter donated it to the National Air and Space Museum. The passport containing the positive of this image remains in the collection of the Missouri Historical Society.

023

**GILMORE** Roscoe Turner, the flamboyant air racer of the 1930s, winner of the Bendix Trophy and three-time winner of the Thompson Trophy, was a natural at self-promotion. The debonair pilot sported elaborate uniforms and wore his mustache waxed — but it was a lion in the cockpit that attracted the most attention. While flying under the sponsorship of the Gilmore Oil Company, whose logo was a lion, he had the brilliant idea of using a lion as his copilot for a publicity stunt.

The lion, appropriately named Gilmore, was three weeks old when Turner acquired him. As a young cub, Gilmore was terrified upon takeoff and always scrambled into the lap of whoever was sitting in the cockpit. Eventually he grew to enjoy flight and traveled more than 25,000 miles with Turner. A small Irvin parachute was custom-made for Gilmore in case of an emergency. The Humane Society had wondered about the cub's safety, but the parachute seemed to relieve any concerns. The ripcord of Gilmore's parachute was attached to the airplane. In the event of a crisis, the lion was to be thrown out first and his parachute would automatically open. Fortunately, the parachute never had to be used. Gilmore caused a sensation at airports, and one time a hotel manager even stamped the famous mascot's paw print in the hotel registry to document his stay.

Gilmore retired from the cockpit when his weight became a hazard. However, the friendship between man and beast was everlasting. Turner provided the means for Gilmore's upkeep until the lion's death in 1952 at the age of twenty-two and a weight of more than six hundred pounds. The endearing companion was preserved by a taxidermist and remained in the pilot's home until his own death.

**WILEY POST'S MAP AND STRATO-SPHERE SUIT** The colorful story of Texan Wiley Post began in 1914, when he was fifteen years old and saw an airplane for the first time at a county fair. He later set to work in the oil fields of Oklahoma to earn money to buy an airplane and become a barnstormer. In 1921, his wilder side was revealed when he stole a car and was sentenced to ten years in prison. Paroled after a year, he went back to the oil fields. He later lost his left eye in an accident, but, as fate would have it, he was able to use the settlement to buy his first plane. His one-eyed vision didn't inhibit his flying. Eventually, he became a private pilot for oilman F.C. Hall. Post used Hall's Lock-heed Vega *Winnie Mae* to fly twice around the world and later into the stratosphere.

In 1931, accompanied by Harold Gatty as navigator, Post set an around-the-world record of eight days, fifteen hours, and fifty-one minutes. On June 23, they flew from New York, via Newfoundland, England, Germany, Russia, Siberia, Alaska, and Canada, stopping in Cleveland before returning to New York on July 1, traveling 15,474 miles.

Two years later, beginning on July 15, 1933, he repeated his around-the-world flight, but this time alone. With the aid of a Sperry Gyroscope autopilot and a radio compass, he beat his previous record, circling the globe in seven days, eighteen hours, and forty-nine minutes. A crowd of 50,000 people gathered at Floyd Bennett Field in New York to greet the first person ever to solo around the world.

Prior to his solo flight, Post requested maps and assistance in plotting his course from the U.S. Navy Hydrographic Office, Division of Air Navigation. He used this map, showing Buffalo, New York, on his final dash across the North American continent toward New York City.

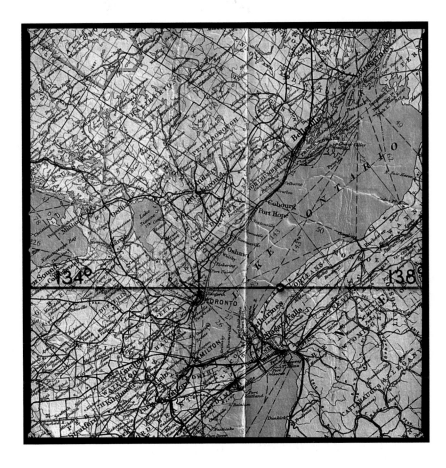

Flying was never too high or too fast for Post. Before planes had pressurized cabins, pilots needed pressure suits to survive the rigors of high-altitude flying. Post conceived a stratosphere pressure suit consisting of two layers: an inner air-containing all-rubber suit and an outer stress-resistant fabric suit with leather boots and gloves. The aluminum head covering with removable window of safety glass was patterned after a diver's helmet. Breathable air was provided by doubled-walled vacuum bottles containing liquid oxygen. As the super-cold gas boiled off, it also pressurized the suit. Engineers at B.F. Goodrich helped Post build it.

On September 5, 1934, his first flight wearing the suit, Post ascended 40,000 feet over Chicago. With modifications to the *Winnie Mae*, including superchargers to provide more pressure to the flight suit and engine, he set an unofficial altitude record of 50,000 feet and discovered the jet stream in the stratosphere. In March 1935, Post used the jet stream to help fly the *Winnie Mae* 2,035 miles from Burbank, California, to Cleveland, Ohio, in seven hours and nineteen minutes, almost two hours faster than James Doolittle's 1931 record. Although his aircraft's top speed was 179 miles per hour, the jet stream boosted his average ground speed to 279 miles per hour. At times, his ground speed exceeded 340 miles per hour. Four transcontinental stratospheric attempts ended in aircraft malfunctions.

Post's stratospheric suit was the first step in pressurized flight, leading to the creation of full-pressure suits for both aircraft and space. He made ten flights in the suit before his death on August 15, 1935. While he was on a leisure trip around the world with comedian Will Rogers, they both died in a crash near Point Barrow, Alaska, when the engine of their modified Lockheed Orion failed shortly after takeoff.

**COMBAT FLAG** On November 14, 1910, pilot Eugene Ely flew a Curtiss pusher biplane from a specially built platform on the USS *Birmingham*, in the coastal waters off Hampton Roads, Virginia. This was the first American aircraft launched from a Navy warship. On January 18, 1911, Ely made the first ship landing, on the deck of the USS *Pennsylvania*, anchored near San Francisco. It wasn't until April 1914, however, that Navy aircraft were called into battle.

This came about when strained relations between the United States and Mexico led Mexican police in Tampico to place U.S. Navy personnel under arrest. The United States reacted by sending Marines and naval forces ashore at Vera Cruz. On April 25, 1914, air detachments from the USS *Birmingham* and USS *Mississippi* (five aircraft and seven pilots) conducted a series of reconnaissance flights over Mexican positions. The aircraft flew scouting missions five to twelve miles inland at low altitudes, making photographs, sketches, and notes. Pilot Lieutenant Patrick N.L. Bellinger, leading the *Mississippi* detachment, suffered several rifle bullet holes to his Curtiss C-3 aircraft while flying near Vera Cruz with assistant pilot and observer Lieutenant R.C. Saufley — the first combat damage to an American aircraft. Bellinger carried this thirteen-star American flag in the airplane.

During World War II bombing missions, flight crews removed these magnesium safety pins from bombs during flight before releasing them over a target. (The bomb remained unarmed while the pin was in place.) Crew members often linked hundreds of safety pins together on a chain as keepsakes. It was common to give a rookie pilot a safety pin on his first combat mission for good luck.

**AIRMAIL BAG** Richard E. Byrd carried the first official U.S. transatlantic airmail. Byrd, acting as navigator for the flight and sworn in as an airmail officer, departed from New York bound for Paris in his airplane *America* on June 29, 1927, with a radioman and two pilots. The crossing went smoothly, but unexpected bad weather surrounding Paris made for a hazardous landing. On the evening of July 1, pilot Bernt Balchen (later to become chief pilot for Byrd's flight over the South Pole in 1929) brought the plane down in shallow water off the coast of Ver-sur-Mer, France, without casualties among the crew. The contents of the salvaged mailbag were properly delivered.

Careful examination of the mailbag by Smithsonian curators discovered two canceled five-cent stamps in the seam folds. The stamps had washed off their parcels when the *America* ditched into the sea.

**MESSAGE CAPSULE** In 1917, with the U.S. entry into World War I, planes from Chatham's Naval Air Station patrolled the Eastern seaboard to guard against German submarines and to keep the waters of Massachusetts Bay and Nantucket Sound secure for American shipping and the critical fishing industry. Navy planes (Curtiss R-9s on twin floats and Curtiss HS-1L flying boats) always went out on patrol in pairs. One carried a radio transmitter, but both had carrier pigeons on board for emergency communication with the base. Each plane carried two pigeons in small wooden cages.

When set free, the pigeons carried messages written on rice paper back to base in lightweight 1¼-inch aluminum capsules. Flexible metal clamps attached the capsules to the pigeons' legs. The birds usually brought news of a broken engine, cracked hull, or ruptured fuel line.

Carrier pigeons had a range of two hundred miles the first year, and twice that distance after two years on the job. Their flights were limited to daylight and good weather, as they navigated by sight. In some instances, the birds would stray off course and head inland. Advertisements would run in local newspapers for the return of pigeons with the marking "N.A.S." on their metal tags, as they were valuable recruits to the cause.

**ANITA THE SPIDER** As a student experiment, seventeen-year-old Judy Miles from Lexington, Massachusetts, suggested that the web-building behavior of a spider be observed in space. Since spiders use their own weight in the process of spinning webs, it would seem that they need gravity. NASA selected her proposal, and two spiders were flown aboard Skylab 3 in 1973.

Arabella and Anita were chosen from approximately 250 candidate spiders for the experiment. They arrived at Marshall Space Flight Center, in Huntsville, Alabama, still in their cocoons. Both were female common cross spiders (*Araneus diadematus*), selected because the species is well documented and female spiders are typically more prolific web builders. The spiders were four months old when Skylab 3 launched on July 28, 1973, with astronauts Alan Bean, Dr. Owen Garriott, and Jack

Lousma also on board, for a fifty-nine-day spaceflight.

Arabella, the prime spider for the experiment, was released into a holding cage. Crew members watched while a movie camera broadcast her web-spinning activity back to Earth. At first the web was asymmetrical, but once she adapted to the environment she constructed normal webs. One noticeable difference was that her thread was finer in space. After thirty days in space, the backup spider, Anita, was let out to get busy. Anita had had more time to adjust to weightlessness and therefore had an easier time of it.

Both spiders perished from lack of nutrition, Anita while still in space and Arabella in her flight "travel vial" when she returned home. The cost of the spiders to NASA was twenty-five dollars.

**SPACE SCRABBLE** Skylab, the refurbished third stage of a Saturn V launch vehicle, was launched into Earth orbit in May 1973. The space station served as both home and research laboratory to three different crews of astronauts. They lived and performed experiments on Skylab for periods lasting twenty-eight days, fifty-nine days, and eighty-four days. It was the first U.S. project for long-duration spaceflight and proved that astronauts could work and live in a zero-gravity environment. Skylab was occupied sporadically until February 1974 and reentered Earth's atmosphere in 1979, scattering debris over Western Australia.

Skylab crew members were normally scheduled to work more than ten hours a day, with duties ranging from scientific experiments to general maintenance. The flight plan included "off-duty" days, when they could relax and take a break. Skylab was equipped with an "Off-Duty Activities Equipment Module," in which exercise gear, reading material, taped music, and games were stored. The astronauts selected their music and books before the flight, and games included playing cards, Velcro darts, and Nerf balls. Most tended to read books, listen to music, or look out the window when they had leisure time.

These Scrabble letters are backed with magnets to prevent them from floating off the game board in zero g. The game was considered for Skylab but probably not flown.

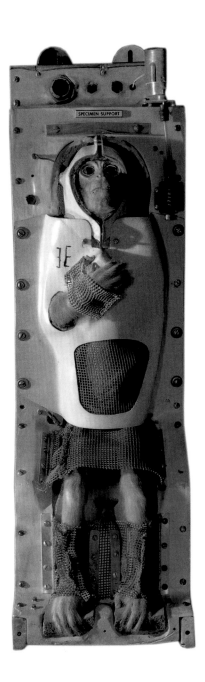

**ABLE** Animals first entered the new frontier of space in 1949, when the U.S. Air Force launched monkeys into the upper atmosphere in a V-2 rocket. The first living creature to orbit Earth was the dog Laika, who spent seven days aboard a Soviet Sputnik satellite in 1957. Animals were used to investigate the effects of space travel on life processes before the manned space programs. Sadly for most animal astronauts, their trips were one-way.

The first successful live recovery of animals from space was accomplished by the team efforts of the U.S. Army and U.S. Navy. On May 28, 1959, two female monkeys, Able (for specimen A), a rhesus monkey, and Baker (for specimen B), a squirrel monkey, were launched into space on an Army Jupiter Missile AM-18 from Cape Canaveral, Florida.

Inside the nose cone, Able and Baker endured their flight within specially designed bio-capsules that provided life support and monitored their reactions to noise, acceleration, deceleration, vibration, rotation, and weightlessness. They rode to an altitude above 300 miles and a distance of 1,500 miles. They were in a weightless environment for about nine minutes and withstood thirty-eight times the normal pull of gravity.

The flight lasted about sixteen minutes, and both monkeys returned safely to Earth. Four days later, Able died from the effects of anesthesia during the removal of her electrodes. Baker died in 1984 of kidney failure at the age of twenty-seven.

The Able-Baker experiment demonstrated that mammals could survive weightlessness in an artificial life-supported environment, and it was a crucial step toward putting humans into space.

**HUMAN PICKUP HARNESS** The first human to be picked up by a moving airplane was paratrooper First Lieutenant Alexis Doster on September 4, 1943, at the Clinton County Army Airfield at Wilmington, Ohio. Wearing a modified parachute harness, crash helmet, and goggles, Doster waited as the aircraft came straight at him at 130 miles per hour. He described the experience as "like that of getting away fast from a standing start with a high-powered motorcycle."

The technique of the human pickup was based on the same principle and equipment that were used in the late 1930s and 1940s for mail pickup in remote communities. Incoming mail was dropped. Outgoing mail was placed in a container that was grabbed by a hook protruding from the belly of a Stinson Reliant Monoplane. The hook engaged a loop supported by two poles, in the position of a goal post. A winch located in the cockpit then drew the mailbag up to the cabin.

Prior to Doster's initial ascent, 126 trial pickups were made with dummies, cargo, and live sheep. The U.S. Army developed a secret program for possible use in rescue efforts. The idea was that packaged kits with simple instruction booklets and pickup equipment (harness and two poles) could be dropped by parachute to stranded servicemen. The program was canceled due to the costs involved and the extensive pilot training that was necessary for safe pickups.

The pilot for Doster's pickup, Captain Norman Rintoul, donated this pickup harness (possibly a later modified version) to the Smithsonian, along with his Stinson Reliant SR-10F, the first plane to make a human pickup.

## JIMMY DOOLITTLE'S FLYING GOGGLES

James H. "Jimmy" Doolittle was a hero many times over. He was acknowledged for his technical advancements as a test pilot, for his long-distance flight records, and for his leadership during World War II. As a pioneer of blind flying, he made the first flight from takeoff to landing by instruments in 1929, proving that flying was safe in all weather. In 1942, he led a famous carrier-based aerial raid on Tokyo with B-25 Mitchell bombers, a feat that earned him the Congressional Medal of Honor. Earlier, Doolittle had also been a champion air racer, winning three of the most important races: the Schneider Marine Cup, the Thompson Trophy Race, and the Bendix Trophy Race.

The first Bendix Trophy Race, in 1931, was the beginning of a yearly "free-for-all" cross-country competition, backed by Vincent Bendix, who believed it would stimulate technical progress within the aviation community. Flying from Burbank, California, to Cleveland, Ohio, Doolittle finished first in a Laird Super Solution in nine hours and ten minutes. After a brief stop-over in Cleveland, he flew on to Newark, New Jersey, thus break-ing a previous transcontinental record and becoming the first to fly across the country in under twelve hours.

These flying goggles were left by Doolittle in a Cleveland restaurant shortly after the Bendix race. They were donated to the Smithsonian in 1972 with Jimmy Doolittle's permission.

## JOE DOOLITTLE'S SIGNATURE TABLECLOTH

Joe Doolittle, Jimmy's wife, first thought of making a signature tablecloth to record the visits of famous friends in 1918. In a letter written to the Smithsonian, she explains, "My husband could not visualize it and highly disapproved."

"In 1928 we were ordered to old Mitchel Field, Long Island, New York. My husband was loaned to Mr. Harry Guggenheim to work on blind flying. So many people passed our way. One day I went into New York City and bought the plainest cloth of linen damask . . . 2½ yard[s] by 3½ — hemmed it — and began to use it."

The night of the first signature, by Jerry Land in September 1929, coincided with the success of the blind-flying project — the first time an aircraft flew from takeoff to landing by instruments. "I asked him [Captain Jerry Land, USN, who was working on the blind-flying project] to sign the cloth with a soft pencil. Trying to preserve the character of the signature I embroidered the name . . . so the cloth was born — to my husband's disapproval. It grew — names were added, often all the guests at a dinner party. Only people who broke bread (ate with us) were asked to sign."

In all, more than five hundred signatures were added to the tablecloth, including famous pilots (for example, Hap Arnold, Ruth Nichols, John Macready, and Marty Laird), movie stars, politicians, scientists, family, and friends. Orville Wright's signature is the only exception to the tradition. A friend took the cloth to him. "We know Mr. Wright — and he did not break bread with us."

"By the way, when we had about one hundred names my husband became very proud of it and assured many that he worked his fingers to the bone embroidering it."

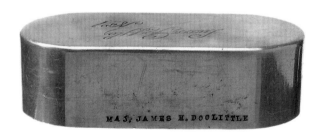

## ALTITUDE CORRECTION COMPUTER

The flight performance of any aircraft can be significantly affected by air density. Because air density varies according to the pressure altitude, temperature, and humidity, an aircraft traveling even short distances can experience very different performance regimes. To describe the atmospheric conditions experienced during a flight, pilots use a term called "density altitude," which is the altitude in the standard atmosphere where a given air density would exist. As an example, when atmospheric pressure, temperature, and humidity decline, the air density decreases and the corresponding density altitude increases. Because of variations of temperatures and pressure, the density altitude on a given day at any given pressure altitude may be several thousand feet higher or lower than the standard atmosphere. One way of determining the density altitude for a specific temperature and

pressure is with a flight or navigation computer.

In the past, there were many different analog flight computers available to pilots and crew that allowed them to make in-flight instrument corrections crucial to the performance of their aircraft. Nowadays, many of these functions can be configured more easily and accurately with on-board or handheld digital equipment. The National Air and Space Museum has numerous analog flight computers, including linear and circular slide rules measuring everything from ordinary temperature conversions and fuel consumption to the extraordinary propulsion calculation for a Saturn V rocket or the ground effects of a nuclear bomb. This altitude correction computer with glow-in-the-dark guide numbers was probably used in the 1940s.

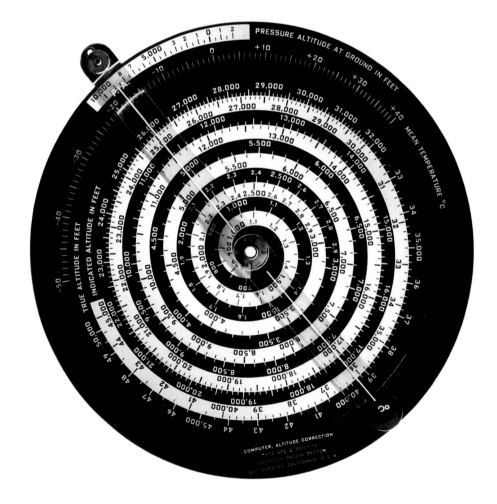

**BOOMERANG** The boomerang is an ingenious device that dates back more than 15,000 years. It seems to have been invented independently by various peoples around the world. Aboriginal communities in Australia are known to have used it for hunting, for sports, as a digging tool, and as a percussion instrument in ceremonies. Boomerangs come in many sizes, are generally made of wood, and can fly more than 650 feet.

A boomerang is an airfoil with two wings. When the boomerang is thrown in a forward vertical spin, the air moves over the wings and creates lift. The boomerang stabilizes its motion during flight by spinning around its center point (or axis), which is the middle of the wings. During its flight, the two wings experience different amounts of lift. As one wing moves forward it enters undisturbed air, but as it continues to spin it enters air disturbed by the other wing. If it were not spinning, these differences would cause the boomerang to flip out of control. Because it is spinning it is able to remain stable, but the forces cause the flight path to curve. Thus, the boomerang will always return if thrown with a proper spin.

This boomerang was made in Western Australia.

## SPACE SHUTTLE *ENTERPRISE*

*Enterprise* (OV-101) was the first full-scale Space Shuttle orbiter, weighing 150,000 pounds and measuring 122 feet long with a 78-foot wingspan. Built by Rockwell International, it was rolled out of its assembly facility in Palmdale, California, in 1976, and towed by truck to NASA's Dryden Flight Research Center at Edwards Air Force Base in 1977. There it completed a series of flights from the top of a specially modified Boeing 747 to test approach and landing systems and determine its glide characteristics.

The Space Shuttle consists of three separate elements: an orbiter with three main engines, two solid rocket boosters, and an external tank holding propellants for the three main engines. Unlike previous spacecraft, the orbiter and solid rocket boosters can be reflown. The orbiter serves as crew quarters and a laboratory, and it can be used to rendezvous with, deploy, and repair satellites in Earth orbit.

NASA had planned to name the first Space Shuttle *Constitution* (in honor of the nation's bicentennial). However, in response to a petition from *Star Trek* fans, it was named after their adored starship, the USS *Enterprise*. In 1985, NASA transferred *Enterprise* by way of 747 to the Smithsonian Institution's National Air and Space Museum.

Although an important test vehicle, *Enterprise* was not equipped to fly in space. Instead, the first flight of the Space Shuttle was conducted by her sister ship, *Columbia*, in 1981. Over the next decade, four additional orbiters were introduced: *Challenger*, *Discovery*, *Atlantis*, and *Endeavour*.

While in the Smithsonian's possession, *Enterprise* has continued to serve as a test vehicle. Following the *Challenger* accident, *Enterprise* was used to test modifications to the orbiter's landing and crew-escape systems. In 1996, Space Shuttle engineers evaluated the internal structure of *Enterprise*, and they were back again in 2003 after the tragic loss of *Columbia*.

**USS *ENTERPRISE*** The four-inch Lucite block containing a miniature model of the USS *Enterprise* was used during the filming of the television show *Star Trek*'s "Catspaw" episode, broadcast in October 1967.

In the episode, an alien named Sylvia demonstrates her magical powers to Captain Kirk and his landing party by waving a model *Enterprise* above a candle flame. At the same time the real *Enterprise* experiences dangerously high heat. Just before the *Enterprise* is about to be destroyed, Kirk removes the model. To prevent the landing party from returning to the ship, Sylvia's cohort encapsulates the *Enterprise* model in glass, which causes the actual *Enterprise* to be surrounded by an invisible force field from which it cannot escape.

The episode, which featured scenes with a black cat, a cobweb-draped castle, and three witches, was *Star Trek*'s attempt at a Hallow-een special. It was also the first episode to introduce the Russian character Ensign Pavel Chekov.

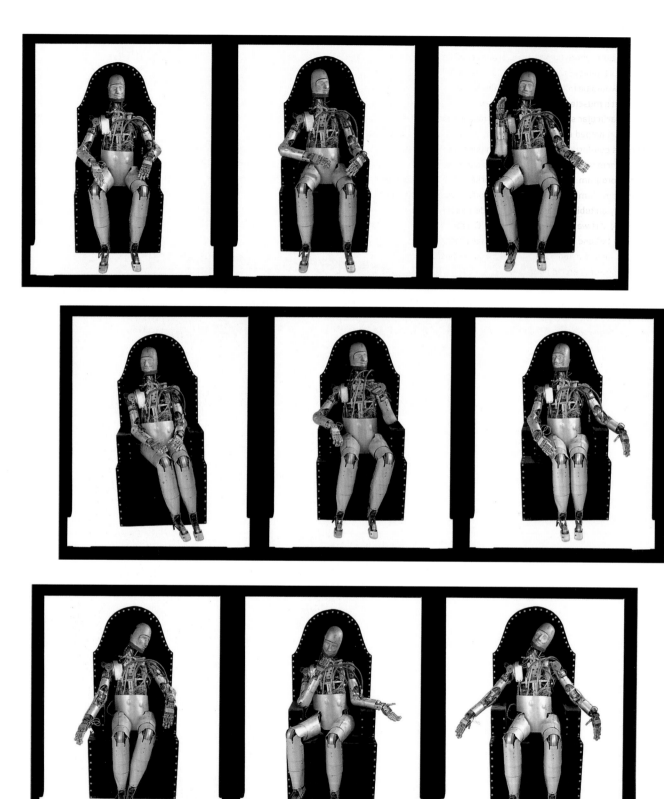

**ART** Art, the anthropomorphic android, was an articulated test dummy designed by the Illinois Institute of Technology Research Institute for NASA in 1963. He worked for NASA's Johnson Manned Spacecraft Center's Crew System Division, where he provided measurements of the stress forces that would be imposed on an astronaut's muscles while wearing a particular spacesuit. Data from Art helped engineers design more comfortable spacesuits and thermal garments for the Gemini program.

Made from aluminum, stainless steel, nylon tubing, brass, and copper wires, Art was slightly less than six feet tall and weighed two hundred pounds. A nylon-tube circulatory system carried lightweight oil to his extremities at a pressure of 1,000 pounds per square inch, and an electrical nervous system controlled valves that opened and closed to direct the oil to hydraulic actuators, allowing Art to perform thirty-five manlike motions, such as clench-ing his fist, bending and rotating his waist, or rolling his head. He was capable of moving his arms forward with a torque of 850 pound-inches, of bending forward at the hips with 2,766 pound-inches, and shaking hands with almost 300 pound-inches. Sensors located at thirty-six joints between the feet and fingertips indicated how much stress was developed in his mechanical limbs during any given movement, thus allowing engineers to test a spacesuit's resistance to motion. When Art worked too hard, he leaked oil, so he often had to sit with an oil pan underneath him.

Current androids in the U.S. space program include Fred, a torso made of human bone and plastic organs, with sensors embedded in his body to measure radiation on the International Space Station, and Robonaut, a humanoid robot in the development stages, to be used for spacewalks.

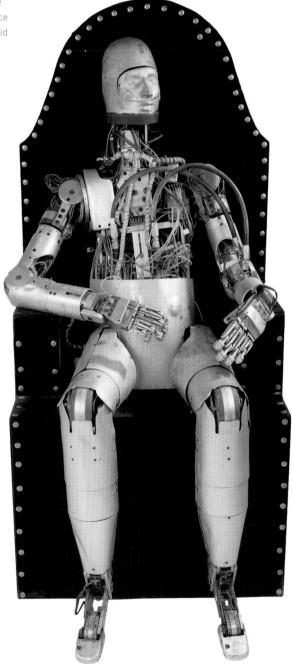

**ED NEU'S LIQUID-FUEL SUPER P ENGINE** This cutaway of a liquid-fuel engine is an early example of the "spaghetti"-type design — so called because the cooling tubes resembled a stack of spaghetti — originally conceived by Ed Neu Jr. of Reaction Motors Inc. (RMI), about 1947. The design was doubly effective: the tubes formed an extremely light yet strong wall to contain the engine's combustion chamber, while the super-cold fuel that circulated through them cooled the engine. Dating from the 1950s, this example was never fired but rather was used to test welding techniques implemented in RMI's Super P engine, a built-in booster for aircraft. The spaghetti concept was a revolutionary development in the history of the liquid-propellant rocket engine and has become an international standard. Among the most prominent examples are the engines for the Saturn V and the Space Shuttle.

**ROBERT GORDON'S LIQUID-FUEL ENGINE** Dr. Robert Gordon of the Aerojet-General Corporation came up with a concept similar to Neu's, completely independently. This early experimental spaghetti-type liquid-fuel-engine chamber design by Aerojet was built in 1948. Gordon used the engine to test gaseous oxygen and hydrogen propulsion with the goal of developing a much larger liquid-oxygen/liquid-hydrogen rocket engine. However, Aerojet General ceased work on the project soon after, and it wasn't until the 1960s that the company developed the Titan missile engine, with an advanced version of this spaghetti type of chamber.

**ROBERT GODDARD'S LIQUID-FUEL ROCKET ENGINE** This liquid-fuel engine is thought to be the first used by American rocket pioneer Dr. Robert H. Goddard for his tests in Roswell, New Mexico, which began in December 1930. In liquid-fuel rockets, the propellants burn in the engine's combustion chamber, producing gases that are expelled from the nozzle. The rocket moves by reaction propulsion. Goddard's rocket, fueled by liquid oxygen and gasoline, reached a height of 2,000 feet.

## AMELIA EARHART'S LOCKHEED VEGA

On the night of June 18–19, 1928, Amelia Earhart became the first woman to fly across the Atlantic — as a passenger. The flight's publicity manager, George Putnam, who later became Earhart's husband, showed he had a good eye when he handpicked the novice pilot, whom he dubbed "Lady Lindy." What he didn't know was that her next goal would be to cross the Atlantic — alone.

With earnings from her flight and publicity tour, she bought a Lockheed Vega 5B later that year. On May 20, 1932, the fifth anniversary of Lindbergh's solo flight, she left from Harbor Grace, Newfoundland, in an attempt to be only the second person, and the first woman, to make the solo transatlantic flight.

From the start, the weather remained a threat, with dense fog. Her altimeter, an instrument that records the plane's height from the ground, failed, and she had to constantly guess at her distance above the dark ocean. If she flew too high, ice and slush accumulated on the wings and window-

panes; too low, and she risked crashing. There was also a gas leak and a crack in the exhaust manifold, caused by the plane's vibrations. The fatigued pilot's only comfort was a thermos of warm chicken soup and a can of tomato juice, which she sipped throughout the flight.

Early the next morning she landed in Culmore, Londonderry, Northern Ireland, after a flight of fifteen hours and eighteen minutes. Earhart's explanation of her motives for undertaking the flight was in keeping with her modest personality, "It was, in a measure, a self-justification — a proving to me, and to anyone else interested, that a woman with adequate experience could do it." Her success was a milestone for women.

The same Lockheed Vega was used again on Earhart's transcontinental flight, made on August 24–25, 1932, from Los Angeles to Newark, New Jersey. It was sold to the Franklin Institute in 1933 and transferred to the Smithsonian Institution in 1966.

### AMELIA EARHART'S GOGGLES

On August 18, 1929, nineteen women pilots lined up in front of their airplanes for the start of the first transcontinental Women's Air Derby, from Santa Monica, California, to Cleveland, Ohio. The first all-women air race was sponsored by the National Exchange Club. It was open to anyone with at least one hundred solo hours of flying and a current pilot license. Comedian Will Rogers, who was at the event, joked about the women checking themselves in their compacts and powdering their noses; the press immediately dubbed the race the "Powder Puff Derby." The women's attire ranged from riding britches to dresses; the planes they flew had both open and closed cockpits. The planes broke down or ran out of gas, pilots got lost, and one, Marvel Crosson, lost her life. However, sixteen of them crossed the finish line on the ninth day, flying 2,800 miles over deserts, mountains, and forests. It was the highest percentage of entrants of any cross-country race who actually finished. The race was won by Louise Thaden, with Gladys O'Donnell in second place and Amelia Earhart finishing third. Reportedly, Earhart wore these aviation goggles during the race.

## TINY BROADWICK'S PARACHUTE

Fifteen-year-old Georgia Broadwick became a parachutist in 1908 when she jumped from a hot-air balloon. Only four feet tall and weighing a mere eighty-five pounds, she often went by the nickname of "Tiny." Tiny made aviation history on June 21, 1913, when she became the first person to parachute from an airplane. The pilot was the famous aviator Glenn L. Martin; the place, 2,000 feet above Griffith Park, in Los Angeles.

Tiny was the most daring of aeronauts. Dressed in the latest of fashionable silks over ruffled bloomers, she would hang from a trapeze-like swing suspended beneath a barnstorming plane. Suddenly the swing would be released, and she would float to the ground on a flat, circular parachute. Because such parachutes offered little or no control, she experienced far too many unplanned encounters with swamps, trees, and roofs. To protect his daughter from bruises and broken bones, Charles Broadwick designed the "coat pack–type" parachute, with a body harness that offered some of the control and safety of more modern parachutes. Later on, billed as "The Doll Girl," a moniker she loathed, and wearing her father's invention, Tiny would thrill crowds with her leaps from the cockpits of soaring planes. Eventually she accumulated more than 1,100 jumps, making her last one in 1922.

In 1964, Tiny donated one of her original 1918 parachutes to the Smithsonian Institution. It was handmade by her father and consists of 110 yards of silk. She explained that unlike modern parachutes, which are shaped from bias strips to give them the strength to withstand jumps from speeding aircraft without tearing, her parachute is shaped from straight pieces of material.

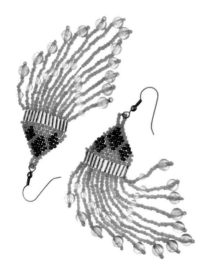

**PATTY WAGSTAFF'S JACKET AND EARRINGS** Patty Wagstaff performs her thrilling, low-level aerobatic routines before millions of spectators at air shows each year. Typical maneuvers include the "snap roll," a high-speed, stalled roll through 360 degrees, and the "rolling 360," consisting of a full 360-degree turn while continually rolling the aircraft a prescribed number of times. Other common maneuvers are described colorfully as the "hammerhead," the "humpty bump," and the "inverted spin." During competition, the entire routine must be flown in a "box" only 3,300 feet by 3,300 feet, with a ceiling of 3,500 feet above the ground and a floor ranging from 1,500 feet to 328 feet, depending on the pilot's ability.

In 1991, Wagstaff became the first woman to win the National Aerobatic Championship since the men's and women's competitions were merged in 1972. She successfully defended the title in 1992 and again in 1993. Before retiring from competition, she was a six-time member of the U.S. aerobatic team, which competes in Olympic-level international competition, and the highest-placing American, with gold, silver, and bronze medals. While performing or competing, Wagstaff could be found wearing these earrings and this jean jacket.

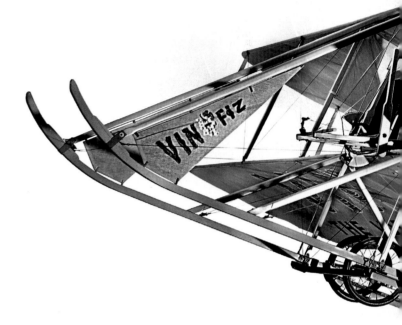

**VIN FIZ** In 1910, a time when only 2 percent of the public had seen an airplane, newspaper mogul William Randolph Hearst offered a $50,000 prize to the first pilot to make a transcontinental flight in less than thirty days. The prize went uncontested for a year, as most pilots considered the feat too dangerous and technologically in-feasible. Finally, in September 1911, adventurer Calbraith Perry "Cal" Rodgers, who had just acquired his pilot's license a month before, stepped up to the challenge with two others.

Rodgers's flight was sponsored by the Chicago-based Armour Company, which was promoting its new grape-flavored soft drink, Vin Fiz. Some said the drink tasted like "a fine blend of river water and horse slop," and even Cal's crew agreed, "You had to sneak up on the stuff to get it down." Rodgers adorned the wings and tail of his new Wright EX biplane with the product's logo — turning the flight

into the first marketing campaign from the air.

Throughout the flight, a bottle of Vin Fiz was tied to one of the struts for good luck. The plane experienced more than a dozen serious crashes and was almost entirely rebuilt by the end of the trip. The two parts of the original structure that survived the journey are the vertical rudder and the one strut to which the bottle of Vin Fiz was attached. Rodgers was the first person to fly coast-to-coast, leaving Sheepshead Bay, New York, on September 17, and arriv-ing in Pasadena, California, on November 5. He had covered 4,321 miles, but since the flight was com-pleted in forty-nine days, he was unable to claim the prize money.

This bottle of Vin Fiz was found in the collection, but it was pro-duced at a later date and by a different manufacturer.

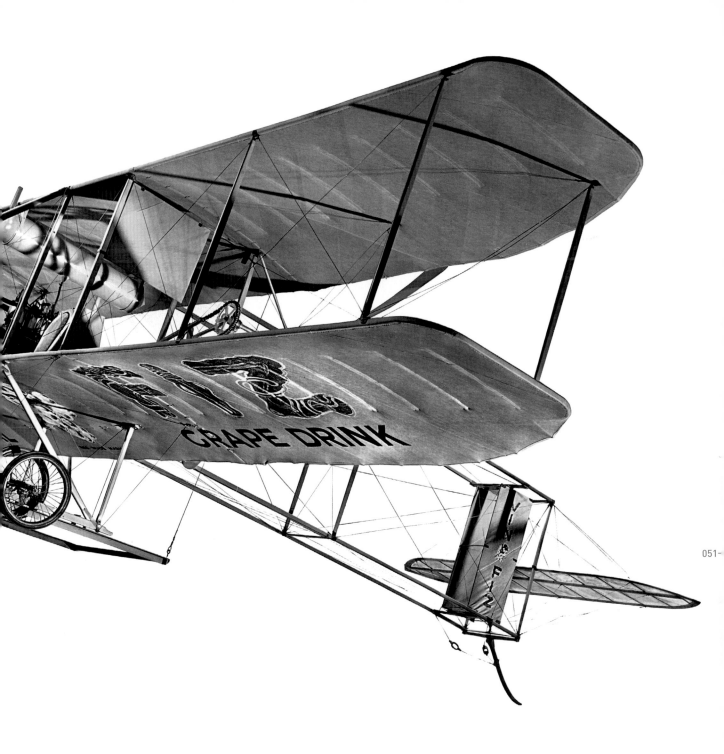

**ASCENSION!** Balloon ascensions attracted thousands of spectators in nineteenth-century America. The inflation process alone was a technological wonder. Many ascensions were turned into spectacles, with dangerous acrobatic acts, balloon-launched fireworks, or animal parachute drops. Until it was realized that onlookers could become paying passengers, the marvel of the balloon ascension was sheer crowd-pleasing entertainment.

This wooden wall-section covered with advertisements for balloon ascensions was discovered during renovations to a home in Prospect, New York, in the early 1990s. The property had belonged to balloonist Harold Squires in the mid-nineteenth century. Squires and his wife, Nellie Thurston, "A Lady in the Clouds," were featured in the ads, as was the American balloonist John La Mountain.

Hailing from Wayne County, New York, La Mountain became famous for his long-distance flight in the *Atlantic* with fellow balloonist John Wise. The flight began in St. Louis, Missouri, on July 1, 1859. The aeronauts traversed Illinois and Indiana, reaching Ohio by the next morning. The *Atlantic* then crossed Lake Erie and the northwestern corner of New York. Finally, it descended over Lake Ontario, but rose again and eventually landed safely in Henderson, New York. The 809-mile journey established a world distance record that stood until 1910. Balloonists in those days must have constituted a small and ingrown community: Nellie Thurston, whose real name was Ellen Moss, was a distant relative and the former wife of La Mountain.

**BUMPER STICKER** As one ABC reporter put it, "Observers of Saturn V rocket launches felt the ground move, and felt the sting of their blouse buttons as they were pressed into their skin by pulsing shock waves emanating from the vehicle's huge engines." The noise produced by the Saturn V rocket engines was at ear-shattering levels of 200 million acoustical watts. The exhaust flames had the apparent brightness of the sun. An ocean of people lined the NASA Causeway, beaches, and highways on July 16, 1969, to observe the launch of Apollo 11 — humankind's first attempt at landing on the Moon.

The rocket, carrying Neil Armstrong, Michael Collins, and Edwin "Buzz" Aldrin, lifted off from Pad 39A at Kennedy Space Center with no launch delays. On July 20, the Lunar Module *Eagle* landed safely on the Moon in the Sea of Tranquility. Neil Armstrong and Buzz Aldrin set a plaque on the surface with the words, "Here men from planet Earth first set foot upon the Moon. July 1969 A.D. We came in peace for all mankind." Their total stay on the lunar surface was 21.6 hours. Splashdown occurred four days later.

This bumper sticker was found in the collection.

**CHARLES LINDBERGH'S *SPIRIT OF ST. LOUIS*** The *Spirit of St. Louis* overcame all odds by carrying its courageous pilot safely across the Atlantic Ocean. Charles Lindbergh had her built to do just that. The small fuselage, just twenty-seven feet long, was loaded with extra fuel tanks, and the forty-six-foot wingspan accommodated the extra-full weight. Emergency equipment, including a parachute and radio, were left behind, and Lindbergh forsook the luxury of a comfortable chair for a lightweight wicker seat. The aircraft, built by Ryan Airlines of San Diego, California, was finished April 28, 1927. It was named in honor of Lindbergh's supporters in St. Louis, Missouri, by Harold Bixby, the head of the St. Louis Chamber of Commerce. He and other business-men funded the flight with $15,000 after Lindbergh convinced his investors that if he *were* success-ful, the historic value of the flight would benefit the city immeasurably. It was just a plane when Lindbergh flew it cross-country on his way to New York; it became an Ameri-can icon when it landed safely at 10:22 P.M., on May 21, 1927, at Le Bourget Field in Paris. It had flown 3,600 miles in 33.5 hours — flawlessly.

The *Spirit of St. Louis* made its final flight less than a year later, on April 30, 1928, to its permanent home at the Smithsonian Institu-tion. Lindbergh wrote to its new keepers, "I would like to have on record in your files of my opposi-tion to moving the plane to any other location for temporary exhi-bition regardless of who makes the request or how worthy the cause may be."

**COCKPIT** The penciled "tick" marks visible at the upper right of the instrument panel were made by Lindbergh as a record and reminder to change fuel tanks every hour. There were five fuel tanks on board, which carried a total of 450 gallons of gas. In order to keep the airplane properly balanced, he had to be sure that the tanks were emptied at an equal rate.

**ENGINE** The power plant of the *Spirit of St. Louis* was a 223-horse-power, air-cooled, 9-cylinder Wright Whirlwind J-5C engine. Lindbergh opted for a single-engine aircraft when other pilots preferred multi-engine aircraft for the transatlantic attempt. His rationale was that one engine would be lighter and more fuel-efficient, and offer fewer chances for trouble. "I'm not sure three engines would really add much to safety.... There would be three times the chance of engine failure."

**FUEL LINES** The plumbing for the fuel system was located directly below the instrument panel in the cockpit. Lindbergh controlled the fuel balance of the five gas tanks by turning these small valves on the fuel lines. The funnel below them caught any excess, which then drained outside the aircraft.

**COWLING** After the *Spirit of St. Louis* was returned to the United States from Europe, Lindbergh took it on a national tour to promote aviation, lasting from July 20 to October 23, 1927. The flags painted on the cowling represented places that he visited during a subsequent tour of Latin America and the Caribbean, from December 13, 1927, until February 13, 1928.

**FLASH GORDON STATUETTE** The high-energy space adventures of *Flash Gordon*, drawn by artist Alex Raymond, arrived on the scene in 1934, during the Great Depression. Youngsters read of fanciful space vehicles, incredible blaster weapons, a beautiful maiden named Dale Arden, and the strange planet Mongo — all of which revolved around the life of Flash Gordon, an Ivy Leaguer from Yale. Cliff-hanging movie serials, a radio show, novels, comic books, and even a U.S. postage stamp were just some of the spin-offs that followed.

King Features Syndicate made this Flash Gordon statuette in 1944.

**PREMIUM RINGS** During the dark years of World War II, children enjoyed the distractions of movies, radio, and the comics. Toys based on popular fantasy characters were offered as "free" premiums by food companies eager to have parents buy their products. It was a great marketing gimmick, and later the toys became collectibles that many adults now associate with childhood memories.

*Captain Midnight*, sponsored by Skelly Gasoline oil products, started as a regional radio program in 1938. By 1940, it was broadcast to a national audience under the sponsorship of Ovaltine, the breakfast drink. The show was about Jim "Red" Albright, a World War I pilot who braved secret missions in enemy territory. He always returned against impossible odds and at the stroke of midnight, hence the name Captain Midnight. The characters included Ivan Shark, Captain Midnight's evil nemesis; Shark's daughter Fury; and his henchman Fang. The series eventually moved from radio to television and film.

Young listeners could become members of a "Secret Squadron" by signing up through Ovaltine. Their membership included a pledge card asking them to be Loyal to the United States, to be Honest at all times, and most important, to be Healthy and drink two glasses of Ovaltine a day. This ring, showing images from World War II on miniature film, is believed to be a Captain Midnight premium from later years.

*Sky King*, a radio show that aired from the mid-1940s to the mid-1950s, was sponsored by Peter Pan Peanut Butter. It too moved to television. Sky was a rancher and detective who flew two airplanes, one called *Song Bird* and the other *Flying Arrow*, and rode a horse named Yellow Fury. Sky King had his own airfield at the Flying Crown Ranch.

One of the *Sky King* premiums is the Magni Glow Writing Ring (with the oval "moonstone" in the center). Inside is a secret compartment with a pen attached.

## DOUGLAS WORLD CRUISER *CHICAGO* AND MAGGIE OF THE *BOSTON*

The U.S. Army Air Service decided to attempt the first around-the-world flight in 1924. Teams consisting of a pilot and copilot were chosen to fly four Douglas World Cruisers that were equipped with specially designed interchangeable landing gears that had both wheels and floats to allow the planes to land on the water or on the ground. The cockpits were outfitted with the standard flight instrumentation of the day, including a compass for navigation. On April 6, the *Seattle*, the *Chicago*, the *Boston*, and the *New Orleans* left Seattle, Washington, and flew west to begin the adventure.

On April 30 the *Seattle* encountered dense fog in Alaska and crashed into a mountainside. Fortunately, the crew survived. The three remaining aircraft continued on to Japan, Southeast Asia, India, the Middle East, continental Europe, England, and Iceland, before returning to North America. The crews prevailed in the face of equipment failures and bad weather that constantly jeopar-

dized the success of the flight. On August 3 the *Boston* was forced to land in the North Atlantic; it was badly damaged while being towed and sank. A Douglas DWC-2 prototype, which the crew promptly named the *Boston II*, was sent to Nova Scotia to replace the lost plane. From there the three planes went on to cross the United States and eventually complete the around-the-world flight by arriving in Seattle on September 28. The total distance traveled was 27,553 miles in an adventuresome 175 days. In addition to capturing the imagination of the public, the triumph of the Douglas World Cruisers demonstrated the promise of air travel to unite the world.

The *Chicago*, piloted by Lieutenant Lowell Smith and Lieutenant Leslie Arnold, is one of the two planes to complete the flight. Paul Garber, a young Smithsonian employee at the time of the flight, foresaw the success of the Douglas World Cruisers, and he began making efforts to acquire one of the aircraft weeks before the flight was over. The secretary of war quickly approved the transfer of the *Chicago*, and it was delivered to the Smithsonian Institution a year later.

While in Los Angeles preparing for the trip, the World Cruiser crews were bombarded with social invitations. Declining most because of their rigorous training and a tight work schedule, they did manage to attend an aviation ball held at the Ambassador Hotel. During the event, the hotel manager plucked eight stuffed monkeys from an artificial palm tree and presented one to each crew member to take as a mascot. The pilots named their monkeys Jiggs, Felix, Petie, Mutt, Jeff, Dodo, Bozo, and Maggie, and brought them along on their journey for good luck.

Luck was something Lieutenant Leigh Wade, pilot of the *Boston*, truly believed in. He was very superstitious and was known to knock on wood six times as a pre-

caution against misfortune. After the *Boston* was forced to land in the North Atlantic, he became angry with his copilot, Lieutenant Henry Ogden, when Ogden walked under a ladder while aboard one of the recovery ships. He seemed to believe that this may have caused the mishap that led to the *Boston*'s sinking.

During the flight, the crews frequently had to jettison excess cargo to decrease weight and save fuel. Wade never threw out his lucky monkey, Maggie. A black velvet pouch tied around her neck reportedly held a silver watch. Wade's signature can be found on her side. Today she continues to bring luck to museum visitors as part of the Smithsonian's collection.

**BYRD RADIO TRANSMITTER** In 1928–30, Richard E. Byrd organized an expedition to explore Antarctica with two ships, three dog teams, and three airplanes. The planes, which included a Ford Tri-Motor monoplane, a Fokker Universal, and a Fairchild monoplane, were to be used primarily for ground surveys and mapping.

Byrd's communication systems surpassed those of previous expeditions, in that radio contact was to be maintained between ships, airplanes, and ground personnel. Prior to the expedition, he had approached Ralph Heintz of Heintz & Kaufman, who built the Weston Thermo-Ammeter radio transmitter. He hoped that since even the dog biscuits for the sled teams had been donated, Heintz would be willing to part with some equipment. Heintz declined. Byrd, who was convinced of the quality of the radios, decided to buy them. It proved to be a wise decision. On January 25, 1929, a distance record was achieved with the Heintz & Kaufman equipment on board the Fairchild *Stars and Stripes,* as the explorers communicated with New York City, 10,000 miles away, using Morse code.

*Stars and Stripes* was buried in the ice and left behind after the first expedition concluded in 1930. It was resurrected in December 1933 and restored to flying condition to support Byrd's second expedition. When the expedition concluded in 1934, it was returned to Brooklyn by boat. In 1935, *Stars and Stripes* was sold with the working transmitter on board. The new owner removed the transmitter from the aircraft in 1937 and eventually sold it back to Ralph Heintz, who later donated it to the museum.

(Although this radio was found aboard the Fairchild *Stars and Stripes,* a clue etched into its front suggests that it may have been the original transmitter from the Fokker Universal *Virginia.* On March 14, 1929, while on the ground in Antarctica, the *Virginia* was destroyed in a storm. The crew members — Larry Gould, Bernt Balchen, and Harold June — were on a geological survey near the Rockefeller Mountains. By March 18, the weather had cleared enough for Byrd, Dean Smith, and Malcolm Hanson to rescue them. Balchen, Smith, and June returned to the base at Little America. They managed to salvage most of the equipment from the wreck but left the transmitter behind because it was too hard to remove. Byrd, Hanson, and Gould stayed behind to wait for an expected second rescue mission, departing the area about March 22. Scratched into the radio from the *Stars and Stripes* are the words, "Left here 3/22/29 Byrd, Gould, Hanson," suggesting that it was the same one left behind in the *Virginia.* The radio could have been removed from the Fokker aircraft on Byrd's second expedition and later installed in the Fairchild.)

**AMELIA EARHART'S RADIO**  On January 11, 1935, less than three years after her solo transatlantic flight, Amelia Earhart departed alone from Honolulu, in a bid to become the first person to fly from Hawaii to the mainland. Her modified Lockheed Vega NR965Y, the same type of plane she had used on her Atlantic flight, was readied at Wheeler Field. Delayed by rain, she began her journey late in the afternoon, at 4:22 P.M., with mostly military personnel watching her departure.

This time she had a radio. Earhart could tune in to the local KGU Honolulu broadcast station. In her book *Last Flight*, Earhart recounted,

I wasn't listening to music as such, but simply keeping the station tuned in so that when word came for me, arranged before hand, I could increase the volume. Suddenly I heard the music stop and the announcer's voice say "We are interrupting our musical program with an important news flash. Amelia Earhart has just taken off from Honolulu on an attempted flight to Oakland. Mr. Putnam will try communicating with his wife." Then I heard my husband say. "AE the noise of your motor interferes with your broadcast. Will you please try to speak a little louder so that we can hear you." It was thrilling to have a voice come in so clear to me, sitting out there over the Pacific.

After three hours of fog, she said into her microphone, "I am getting tired of this fog." The message received was "I'm getting tired." So a nurse and physician were dispatched to the airport at Oakland to revive the exhausted flier when and if she arrived. "Of course I wasn't tired at all. No one should undertake a long flight who becomes fatigued after staying up just one night under normal flying conditions."

She arrived eighteen hours and sixteen minutes later and was greeted by an enormous crowd. The radio broadcasts between the plane and the mainland had alerted the public to Earhart's estimated arrival time. The use of a two-way voice radio over such a long distance was still new for civilian aviation.

061—

**E.T. TRADING CARDS** The Topps bubblegum packet with sixteen collectible trading cards is a souvenir of the 1982 box-office hit *E.T.* Director Steven Spielberg, creator of the extraterrestrial fantasy movie, portrays the friendship between a young boy and an endearing alien who has traveled far from his own planet and becomes homesick after being marooned on Earth. The Earthling shows his love for the creature and tries to rescue him from government agents. The most famous line of the film is spoken by the alien: "E.T. phone home."

On November 16, 1974, a real message was beamed from Earth to any extraterrestrials that might be listening. The message was sent as part of the dedication ceremony of the Arecibo radio telescope in Puerto Rico, and it contained basic information about humankind, including the molecular structure of DNA and a diagram of our solar system. The intent of the message was to demonstrate the remarkable power of a new radar transmitter installed at Arecibo and the capability of the telescope's 2,000-foot-diameter dish antenna. Meanwhile, researchers continually use the huge dish to listen for signals from alien intelligence, but so far nobody has phoned back.

**PERCIVAL LOWELL'S MARS GLOBE** Percival Lowell discovered life on Mars. He interpreted dark lines observed on the planet as water canals leading to areas of vegetation . . . and theorized that someone had to have built the canals. Although his ideas were controversial in the 1890s, they fascinated the general public. The origin of the perennial interest in the Red Planet and its potential for life lies with Lowell's inaccurate science.

Lowell's engagement with Mars came "out of the blue," when he was thirty-eight years old. Born into a family of wealth, he graduated from Harvard with a distinguished record in mathematics, but it would be years before he put this talent to practical use. He thought he found his niche documenting ancient traditions of Japan, and he spent years traveling the Far East. After reading Camille Flammarion's *La Planète Mars* in 1893, Lowell experienced an epiphany. He became determined to find life on Mars. With equipment borrowed from Harvard, he built an astronomical observatory in Flagstaff, Arizona, in 1894. He made his startling claims after only a few months of observing the planet. Lowell studied Mars and other planets from his observatory for another fifteen years.

The Mars Globe made by Percival Lowell in 1901 encapsulated his observations of the planet. It is displayed at the National Air and Space Museum's *Exploring the Planets* gallery and is on loan from Lowell Observatory, today one of the most renowned astronomical research observatories in the world.

H. O. No. 205

# 1929
# RADIO AIDS TO NAVIGATION

## INCLUDING DETAILS OF
### RADIO-COMPASS STATIONS, RADIOBEACONS, WEATHER BULLETINS, STORM AND NAVIGATIONAL WARNINGS, TIME SIGNALS, ETC.

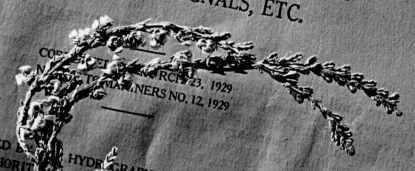

CORRECTED TO MARCH 23, 1929
NOTICE TO MARINERS NO. 12, 1929

PUBLISHED BY THE HYDROGRAPHIC OFFICE UNDER THE
AUTHORITY OF THE SECRETARY OF THE NAVY

### PRICE 75 CENTS

UNITED STATES
GOVERNMENT PRINTING OFFICE
WASHINGTON : 1929

**ANNE MORROW LINDBERGH'S RADIO MANUAL AND CONTROL STICK** Anne Morrow, the daughter of the U.S. ambassador to Mexico, Smith College graduate, and aspiring writer, married Charles A. Lindbergh, aviation hero and most sought-after bachelor, on May 27, 1929, in a private ceremony in her family home in Englewood, New Jersey. As husband and wife, they flew together for leisure, surveyed routes around the world, and broke records, including a transcontinental flight in March 1930 from Los Angeles to New York with Anne seven months pregnant. Anne Morrow became the first woman in the United States to obtain a glider's license, and when she flew with her husband she became the radio operator and copilot. These artifacts celebrate the role she played in aviation.

Anne's memoirs of two flights in the Lockheed Sirius, *North to the Orient* and *Listen! The Wind,* have become classics. *North to the Orient* describes what was supposed to have been a leisure trip, from Maine to the Far East via the Arctic Circle, in the late summer of 1931. By today's standards it was hardly a vacation. The flight took the Lindberghs over the desolate tundra of Alaska and Siberia, and it terminated in China, via Japan, at the end of September. The flight proved the feasibility of flying to Asia from the United States along a great circle route. *Listen! The Wind*

details a survey flight in 1933 that crossed the Atlantic, stopping along the way in Greenland, where the Lindberghs' plane was christened with the Eskimo name "Tingmissartoq," meaning one who flies like a big bird, and proceeding through Europe, Russia, Africa, South America, and the Caribbean. The trip was sponsored by Pan American Airways and was a joint effort by five countries (each flying a different route) to survey potential routes for commercial air transportation.

After completing these trips, the *Tingmissartoq* was given to the American Museum of Natural History in New York City in 1933. It was later transferred to the Air Force Museum in Dayton, Ohio. In 1959 the plane and several crates of equipment were moved to the Smithsonian Institution. The crates contained personal items of the Lindberghs' that included clothing, books, emergency equipment, radio equipment, flight instruments, a rubber raft, food rations, fishing hooks, binoculars, and signed *National Geographic* magazines with articles written by both Lindberghs. These items have been in storage for several years and have recently been rediscovered.

Among them was a radio manual, as well as a pair of gloves and a control stick.

In the planning stages of the trip to the Orient, both Charles and Anne talked about the need for a radio.

Charles asked, 'Can you operate a radio?'

*I can see it coming, I thought, I can just see what's going to happen.* 'A little — I learned at Brooks.'

Then turning to me, he said, 'But *you* will have to be the radio operator.'

The next day he came home with a small practice set of buzzers and keys, connected to two dry cells.... When I pressed down the key, there was a little squeak which brought four dogs and a baby scrambling into my room.

This radio manual has Anne's hand-scribbled notes on the pages that referred to radio call signs from both the Orient and the Atlantic flights. There were also telegrams of weather reports from Canada and Europe. The truly remarkable artifact that has survived throughout the years is a dried pink flower, pressed between the pages.

Anne Morrow often flew the plane from the rear seat to relieve her husband so that he could nap. The control stick and gloves were used on both flights.

## OCTAVE CHANUTE'S ANEMOMETER

The success of the first powered heavier-than-air flight in 1903 was due to exhaustive research, experimentation, the innovative use of new technology, and the interaction of great minds. Among the latter was the French-born Octave Chanute, a civil engineer in the United States who by 1894 had gained international recognition for his research in aeronautics. The Wright brothers discussed their ideas with Chanute and used him as a sounding board as they designed their aircraft.

In the spring of 1900 at Kitty Hawk, the Wrights had used an anemometer (a gauge that measures wind velocities) at the nearby Weather Bureau Station. Requiring an instrument that could be used in the field, Wilbur wrote to his friend Chanute for advice.

Chanute was generous with his knowledge, and in a letter dated March 26, 1901, he replied, "The convenient anemometer for field use is the kind with very light flat vanes. The best is made by Richard in Paris (metric units). I have one of them, also a registering instrument graduated to British measure made in Liverpool. Both have been tested and are proved with a formula for corrections. I will lend them, either you like, when you are ready to experiment." The Wrights accepted this Richard anemometer and attached it to their gliders, which helped them to measure the duration and airspeed of the flights.

**CHARLES LINDBERGH'S FLYING SUIT AND HELMET** There were many facets to the life of Charles Augustus Lindbergh. These artifacts evoke the young aviator. As a boy, he heard an airplane overhead and knew instinctively his home would be in the sky. While in his second year of college at the University of Wisconsin, he dropped out and enrolled in a flying school in Lincoln, Nebraska. There he received his training as a mechanic and learned to fly in a newly purchased Curtiss Jenny. After a short spell of barnstorming, the young pilot entered the U.S. Army Flight School and finished first in his class. The year 1926 would be a turning point, for this was when he perfected and tested his skills as an airmail pilot flying routes between Chicago and St. Louis, often at night and in treacherous weather. And it was when he decided to try for the $25,000 Orteig prize for the first nonstop flight between New York and Paris, which had gone unclaimed since 1919. Lindbergh thought, "Why not?" After all, he was only twenty-four years old. A year later he became an overnight American hero.

Lindbergh wore this wool-lined flying suit and leather helmet between 1927 and 1933.

**SPACE FOODS** It's probably just a matter of time before Starbucks coffee makes its appearance in space. As astronauts spend ever-increasing amounts of time in orbit, their food has become more appealing, no longer consisting of strange-tasting concoctions. Thanks to the commercial food industry, some items can be bought off the grocery-store shelves, and with dietitians creating tastier space foods for NASA, astronauts now have a wider selection of meals available. Menus on board the International Space Station include broiled lobster tails, seafood gumbo with rice, beef teriyaki, and fettuccine Alfredo. Favorites seem to be fresh fruits and vegetables, M&M candies, and Oreo cookies, which are often delivered by new or visiting crews aboard the International Space Station. Astronauts can choose their menus, but the nutritional content must first be analyzed by the Space Shuttle dietitian to provide their recommended daily allowances.

Some foods that still don't work in space are carbonated soda drinks (the carbonation in the soda will separate in microgravity), frozen foods like ice cream (because spacecraft don't have freezers), and foods requiring refrigeration, such as pizza (because they don't have refrigerators). NASA is currently designing a habitat, called Bio-Plex, intended for long flights where all life-support elements will be recycled and reused. Crops of wheat, soybean, potato, peanut, rice, tomato, and sweet potato, as well as various salad greens, will be grown on board.

The early American space foods were typically in a dehydrated form, and the astronauts mixed them with the water generated by fuel cells. These two coffee containers were flown on the first Space Shuttle mission. The Soviets, also coffee drinkers, carried tubes filled with foods that could be heated on board the Soyuz in special "soup" warmers. The tube foods shown here, in addition to coffee with milk, are green cabbage soup and canned chicken.

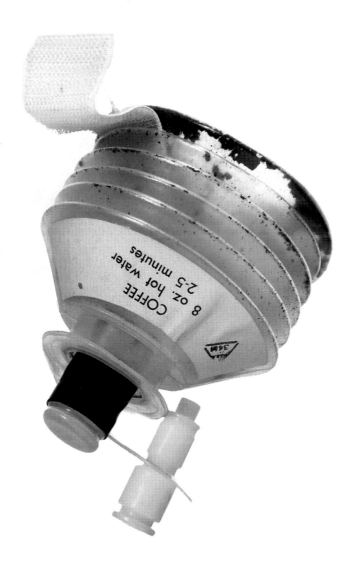

**APOLLO 11 STOPWATCH** History will always remember the three men who accomplished the first lunar landing, but the unsung heroes in Mission Control should not be forgotten. At one point the Apollo 11 mission could have been scrubbed if it weren't for the wits of a twenty-seven-year-old flight controller named Steven Bales. During the final phases of landing, the lunar-module computer began to experience a series of problems resulting in alarms. With the success of the mission on the line and the lives of the astronauts at stake, Bales had to determine the seriousness of the alarms and how to deal with them. Bales said, "Go!" He knew the alarms simply meant that the computer was receiving too much data from the landing radar, and the mission could continue safely.

As the Lunar Module *Eagle* skimmed over the lunar surface, the astronauts realized that the navigational computer was sending them toward a field of boulders adjacent to a very large crater, and Neil Armstrong took manual control. With only two minutes of propellant remaining, the flight controller in Houston, using a stopwatch, began to follow the amount of burn time remaining for the lunar module. Nervously he watched the seconds tick away as the astronauts continued to look for a safe landing site:

HOUSTON: Thirty seconds [of fuel remaining].
*EAGLE*: Contact light! O.K., engine stop . . . descent engine command override off . . .
HOUSTON: We copy you down, *Eagle*.
*EAGLE*: Houston, Tranquility Base here. The *Eagle* has landed!
HOUSTON: Roger, Tranquility. We copy you on the ground. You've got a bunch of guys about to turn blue. We're breathing again. Thanks a lot.

When President Richard M. Nixon presented the astronauts with the Medal of Freedom, Flight Controller Steve Bales received one too. The stopwatch hanging from a shoelace was used by Bales in Mission Control during the descent of the Apollo 11 lunar module.

**ARMSTRONG DIP FORM**  Unlike today's Space Shuttle spacesuits, which come in various sizes for both men and women, the suits designed for the Apollo astronauts were custom-tailored. Each Apollo astronaut actually had three spacesuits that were made especially for him. One was worn in training, another was used for the actual mission, and the remaining suit was reserved as a backup.

The gloves worn on lunar-surface missions were also custom-tailored. The interior of each glove contained a structural restraint and bladder system. The exterior was covered with multiple layers of insulation for protection in case the glove tore or rubbed up against a rough surface. The thumb and fingertips were made of silicone rubber to allow for "touch" sensitivity, which was necessary for handling tools and collecting lunar samples.

Approximately twenty-five Apollo astronauts had casts made of their hands for their personalized gloves. The casts were used by ILC Dover to produce hard-rubber "glove dip forms," like these of Neil Armstrong's hands, which in turn were used to form gloves. There are several different hand forms from the astronauts in the museum's collection.

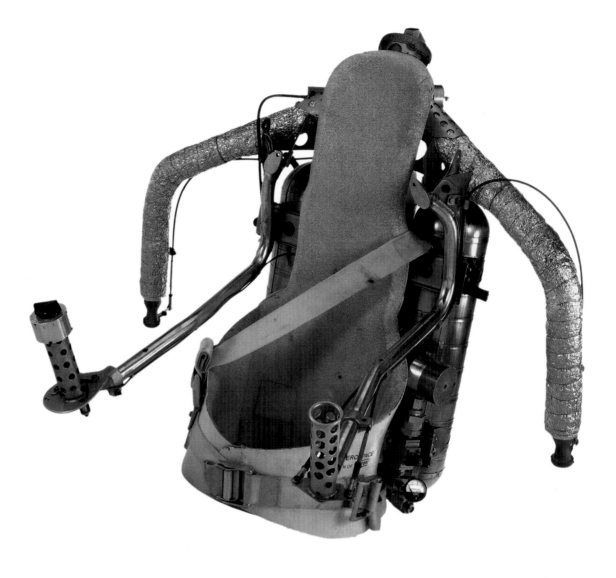

**BELL ROCKET BELT** Fictional concepts of the rocket belt first appeared in the late 1920s as Buck Rogers's mode of transportation in the comic strips. During the 1930s, a young German strapped solid-fuel rockets to his back in an attempt to increase his speed on roller skates, with unfortunate results. Another science-fiction rendition appeared in the 1949 movie serial *King of the Rocket Men*. The inventor of the first wearable flying apparatus was probably Wendell F. Moore, an engineer for Bell Aerosystems, in 1953.

The Bell rocket belt was a metal-frame backpack bearing three tanks filled with non-combustible hydrogen peroxide gas. The operator flew standing upright, with knees slightly bent, always wearing a crash helmet. Tethered to ropes, Moore tested the first rocket belt himself in 1958. In 1959, a successful untethered hop of fifteen feet was made, and it caught the attention of the U.S. Army. The rocket belt was considered for combat soldiers on the theory that it would enable them to leap short distances such as over narrow rivers. The device turned out to be impractical, chiefly on account of the added weight, the very short flight time (twenty seconds), and the loud screeching noise heard overhead as it flew by. Although the military spurned it, the rocket belt was still a popular crowd pleaser in the entertainment industry. At one point Bell Aerosystems had its own rocket-belt demonstration team, which made more than 2,500 public flights around the world.

**FLYING PANCAKE** Sightings of a strange object were reported in the skies above Stratford, Connecticut, in 1942–43. The Vought V-173 "Flying Pancake," often mistaken for a flying saucer because of its unusual appearance, was a low-powered full-scale test model for the top-secret U.S. Navy XF5U-1 Experimental Fighter.

Aircraft designer Charles Zimmerman proposed the world's fastest vertical-takeoff-and-landing propeller-driven airplane, and Chance Vought Aircraft produced a prototype, made of wood and fabric. The aircraft, with its twenty-three-foot-plus wingspan, was nearly circular in shape. The entrance into the cockpit was from underneath the aircraft. In high-speed and cruising flight, it was supported by the fixed wing. At low speeds and while hovering, it was supported by large propellers at the extremities of the wing for forward flight propulsion and, when rotated 90 degrees, to serve as lifting rotors. Although radical in design, its flight characteristics were particularly advantageous for Navy aircraft operating from carriers.

The V-173 was flown for the first time by Vought chief test pilot Boone T. Guyton on November 23, 1942. Over the course of two hundred test flights, a number of Navy pilots, including Charles Lindbergh, flew it. Although the Flying Pancake had many emergency crashes, the pilots were never able to put the airplane into a complete stall or spin, which was, as Guyton once remarked, "a great thing... in a dogfight."

In 1944, the Navy ordered two XF5U prototypes based on the success of the V-173. Built as a fighter and capable of reaching a speed of 500 miles per hour, the XF5U-1 was bigger, more powerful, and fully equipped to carry armament. The Flying Pancake, however, was superseded before it was ever flown. The Navy lost interest in propeller-driven planes with the onset of the Jet Age. It canceled the contract in 1947 and ordered the XF5U-1 destroyed.

With the completion of the program, the Navy approved the transfer of the V-173 to the Smithsonian, where it awaits much-needed restoration. Absent from the tips of each airfoil are two gigantic sixteen-foot, three-bladed wooden propellers.

## AIRCRAFT SPOTTER CARDS

Throughout America and at her outposts overseas, vigilant eyes looked skyward after Japanese aircraft attacked Pearl Harbor on December 7, 1941. With America's entrance into World War II, both men and women in the military and civilian communities were posted to "spotting" towers along the coastal United States and scanned the skies for enemy aircraft. When an airplane was spotted, its type was recorded in a log and reported by telephone to a central plotting bureau.

Airplane spotter cards were produced as learning aids for people whose lives may have depended on their ability to quickly recognize Allied and enemy aircraft from the ground or air. These cards, issued by the Coca-Cola Company, depict aircraft silhouettes from Germany, Italy, Japan, Great Britain, and the United States.

**CURTIS LEMAY'S CIGAR** General Curtis Emerson LeMay was equally famous for his controversial strategic-bombing philosophy during and after World War II and for his cigar-chomping, tough-talking, hardnosed personality. He believed that "every soldier thinks something of the moral aspects of what he is doing. But all war is immoral and if you let that bother you, you're not a good soldier."

LeMay's bombing campaigns ultimately helped win the war. As a group commander in Europe, he designed strategies that enabled daylight bombings to work against Nazi Germany. In Japan, as a B-29 commander, he ordered the ordnance of 325 B-29 planes to be replaced with firebomb clusters and conducted night bombing raids that annihilated several Japanese cities before the deployment of the atomic bomb.

His most important achievement after the war was the redesign of the Strategic Air Command, the Air Force unit responsible for providing the United States with a twenty-four-hour airborne nuclear deterrent. In 1948, when he took command, he was dismayed at the condition of his forces. After years of harsh training that earned him the sobriquet "Iron Ass," he turned the SAC into one of the most powerful and effective military forces in the world. The unit was on permanent alert, ready to deliver what he called his "Sunday punch" — an all-out atomic attack — at the shortest possible notice.

This cigar was acquired through an acquaintance of LeMay's daughter. Reportedly, once while LeMay was smoking one of his cigars inside an aircraft, he was reminded that it might cause an explosion. He replied, "It wouldn't dare." Actually, LeMay rarely smoked his cigars. He chewed them, because of a rare muscle disorder that affected his facial muscles.

**TUSKEGEE AIRMAN GLOVE WITH MEDALS** The story of the Tuskegee Airmen is one of courage, perseverance, and ultimate victory against a background of racial discrimination. Prior to World War II, the U.S. Army Air Corps banned African Americans from flight training, a policy of racial discrimination that existed throughout the world of aviation. With the prompting of his wife, Eleanor, President Franklin D. Roosevelt ordered the Air Corps to create an all-black air unit. The 99th Pursuit Squadron took shape in 1941 at Tuskegee Institute in Alabama, soon to be followed by three additional fighter squadrons to form the 332nd Fighter Group. The Tuskegee Airmen, while segregated into one fighter group, flew with the 15th Air Force in North Africa, Sicily, and Italy during World War II.

The Tuskegee Airmen were led by Benjamin O. Davis Jr., who later became a leader in the post-war Air Force. His 332nd flew hundreds of escort missions, including more than two hundred bomber-escort missions for the 15th Air Force. They decorated the propeller spinners and tail surfaces of their P-51 Mustangs with red paint, earning them the nickname "Red Tail Angels." Although prejudice against the flyers was prevalent, many in the 15th Air Force abandoned their initial hostility toward the Tuskegee Airmen after the 332nd Fighter Group demonstrated their flying skills and bravery.

The Tuskegee Airmen waged two battles simultaneously during World War II. They fought for equality and acceptance in their own country, while defending it from enemies abroad. On July 26, 1948, President Harry S. Truman issued Executive Order No. 9981 desegregating the Armed Forces.

Tuskegee Airman Louis R. Purnell wore this glove and watch in World War II. He flew eighty-eight combat missions with the 99th Fighter Squadron (renamed in 1942), serving two tours of duty in North Africa, Sicily, and Italy. His medals included the Distinguished Flying Cross (not shown). As a civilian, "Lou" acquired many artifacts for the collection of the National Air and Space Museum, where he worked as a curator until his retirement in 1985. The museum lost a colleague and a friend when he passed away in 2001.

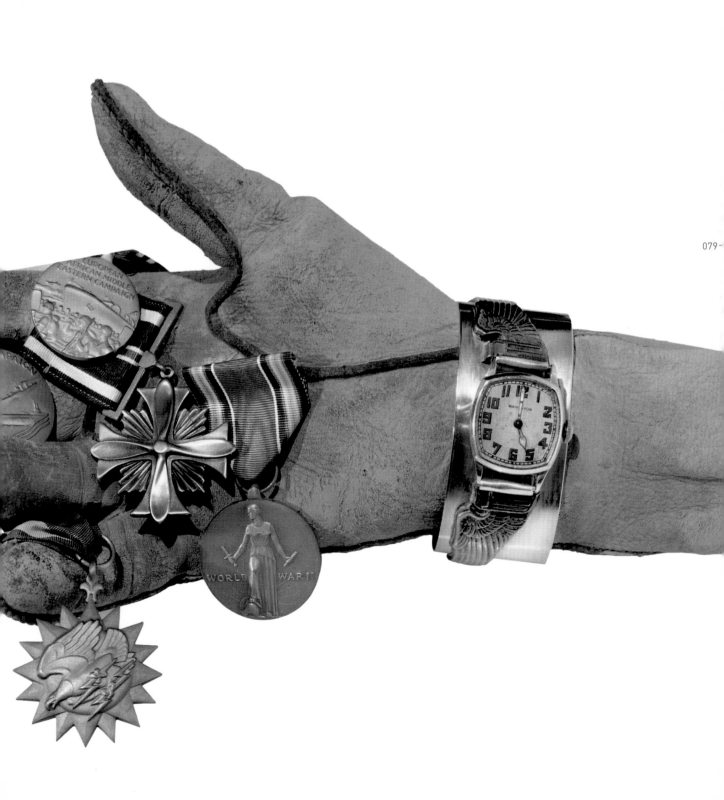

**WILMA DEERING MASK** Science fiction's Buck Rogers, a former World War I Air Service pilot who came in contact with a radioactive gas and fell asleep, spent five hundred years in suspended animation. When he awoke, his first human contact was with Wilma Deering, a twenty-fifth-century American soldier.

Deering was from the futuristic planet of East Central Org. She was young and slender, and had beautiful blue eyes. With her golden hair often hidden underneath her helmet, she patrolled territory vulnerable to the raiding aircraft of the Red Mongols. She fired rockets to give warning of oncoming attacks and was armed with guns to fight them off.

Along with many other social and technological advancements, equality of the sexes came about during Buck's five hundred years of sleep. In the twenty-fifth century, all young girls received military training. They were also educated in various industrial and mechanical trades. Most worked or fought unless they married. After marriage, women adopted homemaking as their career and were called to active duty only in the event of an emergency. Wilma, who was self-reliant and fearless, was a warrior.

The paper mask was made in Japan in 1934.

**JACKIE COCHRAN'S HANDBAG AND GLOVES** With the coming of World War II, women pilots were, for the first time, called upon to fly some of the fastest and largest planes of the U.S. military. The Women's Auxiliary Ferrying Squadron (WAFS) and the Women's Flying Training Detachment were activated in September 1942; a year later (August 5, 1943), they were merged into one organization, the Women Airforce Service Pilots (WASPs). More than one thousand women were selected for the WASPs to release men for combat duty abroad. Wives, mothers, waitresses, actresses, students, and schoolteachers left their normal lives for the opportunity to fly P-51 Mustangs, B-29 Superfortress bombers, and P-47 Thunderbolts.

Jacqueline Cochran, an accomplished pilot and winner of the 1938 Bendix Trophy Transcontinental Race, led the program. Women were trained at Avenger Field in Sweetwater, Texas, the "Army Way" — from early-morning calisthenics to neat (and bobby-pinned) hairstyles, the regimen was a familiar one. The women even wore men's flying suits. Flight school lasted four rigorous months, with classes in math, navigation, physics, and aircraft-engine maintenance. Out of 25,000 applicants, only 1,830 made the cut. In all, 1,074 earned their silver wings. After graduation the ladies were sent off to U.S. Army air bases around the county. Their jobs included testing planes, ferry-ing new planes from factories or damaged aircraft from embankments, and towing banners for artillery practice. The WASPs were underpaid and often encountered discrimination and even harassment. However, they persisted and eventually logged more than 60 million air miles.

Although the WASPs worked for the military, they had civilian status. When a WASP died (and thirty-eight did) their families were denied benefits or a military burial. Instead, the other pilots would pool their money to transport the body home. In 1944, as the war was coming to a close and men began returning home for their jobs, Congress disbanded the WASPs — even though their safety and service records were equal to the men's. In June 1948, Congress established the Women in the Air Force (WAF), with a limited corps of 300 officers and 4,000 enlisted women, but none in pilot roles. The U.S. Navy took the first step in accepting women for pilot training in 1974, with the U.S. Army following suit the same year. The U.S. Air Force caught up two years later. The WASPs were finally recognized in 1979 by the U.S. government and granted veterans status.

Lieutenant Colonel Cochran carried this military fashion handbag and wore these dress gloves.

## PAUL GARBER'S TARGET KITE

In 1941, Paul Garber, a young employee of the Smithsonian Institution, assembled an exhibit of the different types of aircraft flown in the war already raging in Europe, using scale models, photographs, and drawings. Impressed with his display, the U.S. Navy requested that he come to teach the features of both Allied and enemy aircraft to military personnel. Soon thereafter, he was commissioned as a lieutenant in the Navy's Special Devices Airplane Recognition program.

While on the USS *Block Island*, still making models and explaining aircraft, Garber overheard a discussion about the Navy's need for a gunnery target. Normally, the gun crews shot at clouds or banners towed by aircraft, but the results of their marksmanship were often unclear. Garber had an idea. The model maker put together a kite with scraps from the model shop and challenged a gun crew to shoot at it. The target kite showed the results instantly by the number of bullet holes. The

ship's captain was so impressed that he ordered Garber to build a hundred kites.

Garber improved his original concept and created a maneuverable "ship to air gunnery kite" that could loop, dive, climb, and make figure eights, all manually controlled by a reel and harness worn at the waist. The controlled kite could both test and improve the gunner's skills. He even had enemy aircraft silk-screened on the front to provide incentive for the gun crews. The Navy patented the design, and well over 200,000 of Garber's kites were sold.

This five-foot Mark 1–design kite was intended for the Pacific theater of combat in World War II. The aircraft printed on the front is a Japanese Zero.

**JAPANESE KITE** Garber began flying kites when he was five years old. At ten, in 1909, he watched the Wright brothers fly their first military plane at Fort Myers, Virginia. Alexander Graham Bell (a Smithsonian Institution regent) taught the young aviation enthusiast how to rig a kite, and in 1931 Garber wrote a manual on kite flying for the Boy Scouts. As a curator and aeronautical aficionado, he not only collected kites avidly for the Smithsonian Institution but was responsible for the acquisition of the *Spirit of St. Louis*, Wright Flyer, Douglas World Cruiser, Wright EX *Vin Fiz*, and countless other treasures. When storage became a problem for the aircraft, he initiated the construction of the Paul E. Garber Preservation, Restoration, and Storage Facility in Suitland, Maryland, in 1950. It opened to the public in 1977.

In the late 1960s, Garber also started the Smithsonian Institution Kite Festival, which takes place on the National Mall every year. Kites from all over the world are flown, and competitions are held for hand-made kites. There are hundreds of kites in the museum's collection, with a wide range of age, type, and shape. This is a Yakko-dako kite from Japan. Children would usually attach a long strip of newspaper to the lower end to make it easier to fly. It was recently found in the collection and was probably acquired by Garber years ago. Paul Garber continued to work at the museum as historian emeritus until he passed away in 1992 at the age of ninety-three.

**ENOLA GAY BOMBSIGHT** The *Enola Gay* was one of fifteen Boeing B-29s customized to carry and deliver a nuclear bomb during World War II. The B-29 Superfortress was the most modern propeller-driven bomber to fly during the war, but modifications, including new engines, sophisticated bomb-bay doors, and avionics equipment, were necessary to facilitate the mission of the 509th Composite Group.

Colonel Paul W. Tibbets Jr., in command of the 509th Composite Group, piloted the *Enola Gay* (he had named the plane after his mother). The date was August 6, 1945, and the target was the city of Hiroshima, Japan. The crew members inside the cockpit readied themselves with dark glasses moments before the bomb — named "Little Boy" — was dropped, to prevent blindness from the explosion. At the moment of the blast, they tasted lead caused by electrolysis, due to the effect of radiation on the fillings in their mouths. From the air, the atomic mushroom cloud remained visible for more than ninety minutes, until the plane was more than four hundred miles away. On the ground, the results were devastating. Three days later a second bomb, "Fat Man," was dropped by another B-29 named *Bockscar* over Nagasaki. Japan surrendered on August 14, 1945.

The *Enola Gay* was transferred to the Smithsonian in 1949. The plane remained off-site and was sometimes stored outdoors. In 1961, it was disassembled and brought to the Garber Facility in Suitland, Maryland. The restoration project undertaken by the museum in 1984 was its largest ever, requiring more than 44,000 staff hours. Amazingly, the cockpit was missing only a few items and has been fully refurbished to include all of the original instruments and crew stations. Among them is the Norden bombsight. Bombardier Major Thomas Ferebee used this instrument to determine his aiming point: the T-shaped Aioi Bridge over the Ota River, which runs through the center of the city.

**ARMING PLUG** "Little Boy" was armed after takeoff, to prevent it from exploding in case the *Enola Gay* crashed. Prior to arming, three small green wood-handled "safing" plugs were inserted through small holes in the side of the bomb, interrupting the electrical circuitry. At low altitude, the green plugs were replaced with red arming plugs. Once the bomb was dropped, such plugs would form a continuous circuit to the detonator, which fired a bullet of $U_{235}$ into a target of $U_{235}$ at an altitude of approximately 1,900 feet, causing a nuclear chain reaction. Restoration specialist Richard Horigan found this red arming plug in the cockpit behind the radio operator's table during the Smithsonian's restoration of the *Enola Gay*. How it got there and whether it was used in the bombing run on Hiroshima is unknown.

**BUCK ROGERS TOYS** As early science-fiction writers Jules Verne and H.G. Wells inspired such space pioneers as Robert H. Goddard, the character Buck Rogers influenced an entire culture. Rogers was the first spaceman to spawn an industry that included space toys, books, and movies.

Buck Rogers made his debut in 1928 in *Amazing Stories* magazine. The main character in the story "Armageddon 2419" by Philip Nowlan, Rogers was a World War I Air Service pilot transported to a twenty-fifth-century world of marvelous scientific inventions. His comrades included the beautiful Wilma Deering and the valiant scientist Dr. Huer, and he fought battles with evil Mongol Warlords in fantastic galaxies where advanced weapons ("space blasters") were used to maintain the balance of good and evil. In January 1929, the National Newspaper Service syn-

dicated a Buck Rogers comic-strip series by Nowlan and illustrator Dick Calkins. The comic strip ran for more than forty years and led to the radio series of 1932–47, television series airing in the 1950s and 1980s, and movies.

Like other popular comic strips and radio programs, toys associated with Buck Rogers first appeared as premiums from local advertisers on radio shows in the early 1930s. Soon disintegrator pistols, windup toys, costumes, games, rockets, and comic books flooded the market. There are dozens of Buck Rogers toys and related items in the National Air and Space Museum collection. Shown here are an original mock-up of a space gun made of cardboard, a rare pocket watch, a tin windup toy, and a Dixie Cup lid from 1936.

## CHUCK YEAGER'S FLIGHT SUIT

Charles E. "Chuck" Yeager's legendary flight career began on October 14, 1947, when he shattered the sound barrier in a Bell X-1. Launched from a B-29 that took it to an altitude of about 20,000 feet, the brilliant orange *Glamorous Glennis* reached speeds of Mach 1.06, triggering a sonic boom over California's Mojave Desert that proved his accomplishment.

This was but one high point in a distinguished thirty-four-year military career. In 1941, at the age of eighteen, the native West Virginian enlisted in the U.S. Army Air Corps as a mechanic. The teenager who was prone to airsickness became a World War II ace by the time he was twenty-one. During the war, he was shot down and captured by the enemy, but he managed to escape and rejoined the fray. Between 1949 and 1954, he earned a reputation as one of the world's greatest test pilots at Edwards Air Force Base. Beginning in late 1954, he was assigned to command various U.S. Air Force squadrons throughout Europe, the United States, and South Korea. During the Vietnam War, Yeager flew 127 missions, and in August 1969 he was promoted to brigadier general. One of the most celebrated pilots of all time, he retired from the military in March 1975, after flying more than 10,000 hours in over 330 different types of aircraft.

This flight suit was worn by Yeager during his assignment to the 413th Fighter Wing, 1st Fighter Squadron, the "Fightin' Furies," at George Air Force Base, California, where he became commander in 1958. The squadron adopted "Miss Fury" as its emblem during World War II, after a massive P-47 Thunderbolt attack on Japan.

**X-15** Chuck Yeager took the monumental step of breaking the sound barrier, but greater achievements lay ahead with the development of the North American X-15 in 1959. Three rocket-powered research aircraft were built and flown at hypersonic velocities up to Mach 6. The original mission of the aircraft was to obtain data on hypersonic-flight aerodynamics, but the program eventually became a test bed for physiological and psychological reactions in flight conditions beyond the atmosphere. The X-15 was the first aircraft to break through the atmosphere into the fringe of space, and it accelerated the development of the manned space program in the United States.

The X-15 aircraft measured only fifty feet long and had a wingspan of twenty-two feet. The outer shell was made of a nickel-and-steel alloy (Inconel X) that could withstand temperatures up to 2,000 degrees Fahrenheit. The black-painted surfaces helped the plane dissipate heat as it reentered the atmosphere. The directional stability of the aircraft at high speeds was achieved through the design of the tail and leading edges. The engine, developed by the Reaction Motors Division of the Thiokol Corporation, operated on liquid oxygen and anhydrous ammonia and produced 60,000 pounds of thrust. The engine burned almost ten tons of fuel at full throttle in eighty-three seconds. The X-15 was carried to 45,000 feet by a B-52, and once the plane was dropped, the pilot "lit" the rocket engine and accelerated toward space. The landings were made without power.

The first pilot to fly the X-15 was none other than Chuck Yeager's rival Scott Crossfield. Crossfield, who worked for North American, made the first eight flights, beginning June 8, 1959. A total of twelve pilots flew the rocket-powered machine, and a few even earned their astronaut wings during X-15 flights. The X-15 flew 199 flights over a ten-year period, with a world's unofficial speed record of Mach 6.70, set on October 3, 1967, by U.S. Air Force pilot William J. "Pete" Knight.

The X-15A-1 made its last flight in the program on October 24, 1968. It now hangs in the museum's *Milestones of Flight* gallery, across from the *Spirit of St. Louis* and above the Wright Flyer.

091-

**MOTHERSHIP** Are we alone? Not according to motion-picture director Steven Spielberg's 1977 science-fiction blockbuster hit, *Close Encounters of the Third Kind*, about the human encounter with extraterrestrial life. Unlike the aliens of many science-fiction movies of the 1950s, which are depicted as creepy invaders, Spielberg's come in peace. The icon of the movie was their beautiful mothership. The gigantic space-ship hovered over expansive dark fields radiating light from its many-spired cathedral-like structure.

In reality, the mothership was only a small model that delivered a huge impact on screen. It was constructed of plastic and metal and measures only thirty-eight by sixty-eight inches. Designed by Spielberg and Douglas Trumbull, it was built by a team led by model

maker Greg Jein. It was illuminated by numerous lights placed inside it, which radiated through pinholes. There are additional lights on the tips of the antennae and probes. The majority of surface detail came from model-railroad equipment. Jein's team added its own personal touch by placing "hidden objects" on the model that were invisible to the movie viewer. The mothership is adorned with a Volkswagen bus, *Star Wars'* R2-D2 and a TIE fighter, a mailbox, Jacques Cousteau's two-man submarine, two Avenger aircraft, a graveyard, and probably other hidden surprises known only to the model makers.

Spielberg donated the model to the National Air and Space Museum in 1979.

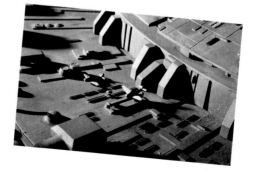

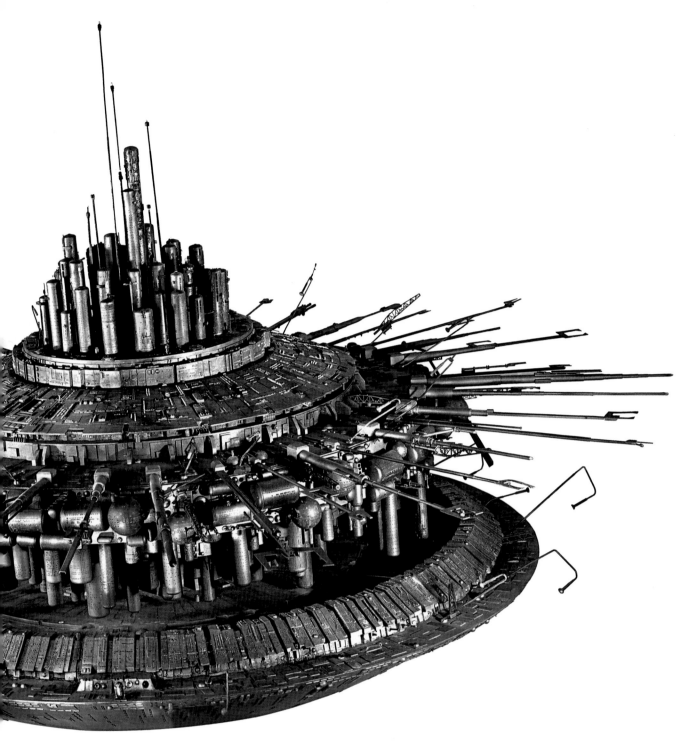

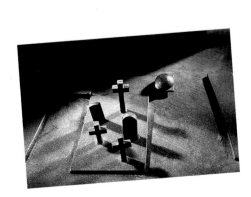

**MILLION-DOLLAR BOX** A primary purpose of the Apollo program was to explore the Moon's surface and return samples back to Earth without contaminating them. Earth's atmosphere contains chemical compounds, such as free oxygen and water, that could have altered the composition of the lunar samples. In addition, scientists weren't completely sure that the Moon did not contain organisms that might be infectious to animals or plants on Earth. To solve these problems, specially designed Lunar Sample Return Containers (LSRCs) were constructed by the Union Carbide Corporation's Nuclear Division in Oak Ridge, Tennessee. To avoid welds that might leak, each container was milled from a solid piece of aluminum. Its lid was sealed with three separate latches. Inside, the box was lined with an aluminum mesh to protect the samples during the return flight. The Apollo 11 astronauts referred to the LSRCs as the "million-dollar boxes." Once safely back on Earth, the boxes were delivered to the Lunar Receiving Laboratory at the Houston Manned Space Flight Center and were opened by scientists under controlled conditions.

The rocks brought back from the Moon varied in composition, size, and shape, but there are three principal types. The most common rock found on the surface are breccias, which are a mixture of other rocks broken up and melted back together during impact cratering. Basaltic rocks account for the dark patches (or maria) we see when we look at the Moon from Earth; these contain iron- and magnesium-rich minerals and were formed from volcanic eruptions when the Moon was still young. Anorthosite rocks, remnants of the Moon's ancient crust, compose its brighter areas. Scientists soon discovered that there was no evidence of living organisms on the Moon and that the rocks would be safe to touch.

The total amount of lunar rock and soil that was retrieved by six Apollo Moon landing missions was 841.5 pounds, most of which is kept under laboratory conditions away from the public. However, in September 1969 the Smithsonian Institution became the first museum to exhibit one of the world's three public samples. The lunar "touch rock" remains on permanent display at the National Air and Space Museum.

This LSRC carried the first lunar samples back to the Earth on Apollo 11, including fifty rocks from the Sea of Tranquility weighing approximately 47 pounds.

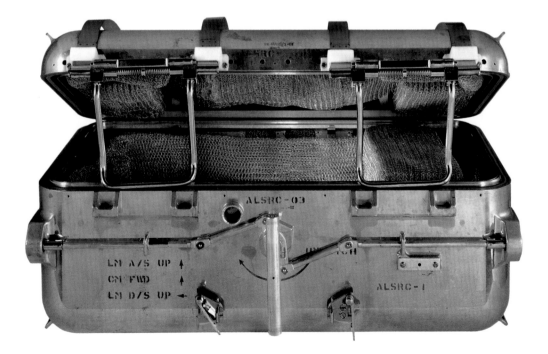

**DOLLAR BILLS** The origin of pilots signing money is not certain, but there is reference to the practice during World War I. Soldiers in that war wrote on paper currency to keep track of names and addresses. They called the bills "short snorters," although how the bills got this name isn't clear. A "snorter" was a drink of liquor swallowed in one gulp. A "short snorter" was a snorter that wasn't quite full. Maybe the soldier who coined the term had downed too many short snorters. Sometimes the bills were taped together, forming a train of short snorters, to add to the confusion.

These dollar bills signed by Apollo astronauts technically were not short snorters. According to a museum legend, each astronaut signed a dollar bill before his flight and put the bill in his pocket. When he came back from space, the dollar bill authenticated that he was the same astronaut who had departed (meaning that little green men hadn't taken the American astronauts and replaced them with aliens). The bills were probably flown as souvenirs or a way to authenticate the flight for the Fédération Aéronautique Internationale.

## APOLLO 13 AIR-FILTRATION DEVICE

About 200,000 miles from Earth aboard Apollo 13, astronauts Jim Lovell, Fred Haise, and Jack Swigert had just finished a live broadcast from space showing Earthlings how comfortably they lived and worked in weightlessness on their way to the Moon. Nine minutes later, Oxygen Tank No. 2 blew up with a loud bang during a routine check. Lovell radioed, "Houston, we've had a problem." Among a list of near-fatal malfunctions, the command module's normal supplies of electricity, light, and water were lost, and that was only the beginning of their unlucky day, April 13, 1970.

With the command module damaged beyond use, the only source of power was the lunar module. Built by Grumman Aerospace Corporation, the lunar module was designed with a modest battery-generated power plant for brief trips from lunar orbit to the lunar surface and back. The crew members powered down the command module and powered up the lunar module; it would be their lifeboat for the trip home. Electrical power was transferred from the lunar module to the command module, a procedure that was the reverse of normal, for the vital reentry operation back to Earth.

Once they were in the lunar module, another serious problem developed: carbon dioxide in the cabin air began rising to poisonous levels. The life-support equipment of the lunar module was, of course, designed to remove carbon dioxide from the spacecraft. The operation required the use of lithium hydroxide canisters as filters, however, and these had to be replaced periodically. Since the lunar module had been designed with life sup-

port for only two astronauts and it was now housing three, the canisters would have to be changed more frequently. Theoretically, these could have been taken from the command module, which had a similar system. The problem was that the command-module canisters would not fit into the lunar-module environmental system's equipment, because different vendors manufactured them and they were of a different size and shape.

Mission Control was determined to get the crew home safely. With their detailed understanding of flight hardware, engineers on the ground improvised a solution using only items that were available in the spacecraft. They designed a supplementary carbon dioxide removal system with an ingenious combination of space-suit hoses, cardboard, plastic stowage bags, and the command-module canisters, all held together with duct tape. They radioed the instructions to the crew, and it took the astronauts one hour to build their new filtering device.

This canister was fabricated at the Johnson Space Center and is identical to the one used on the Apollo 13 mission. The canister fabricated by the astronauts, which provided life support in the lunar module during the return flight, was not recovered.

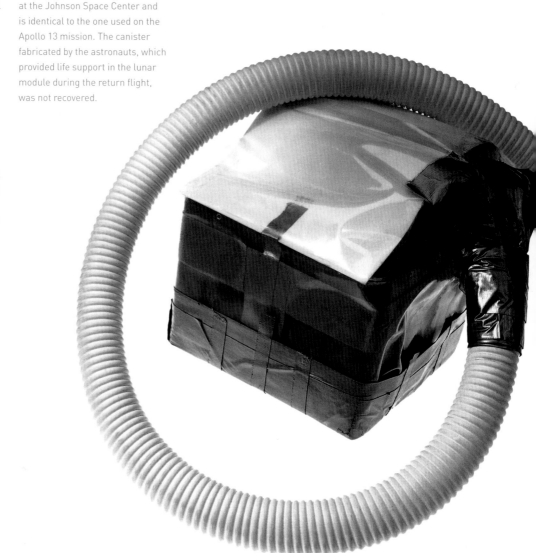

*INVOICE*
~~PURCHASE REQUISITION~~

**A441066**

| DO NOT WRITE IN THIS AREA—FOR PURCHASING USE ONLY | | | | | BUYER | | | | DO NOT WRITE IN THIS AREA—FOR PURCHASING USE ONLY | | | |
|---|---|---|---|---|---|---|---|---|---|---|---|---|

SELLER INVITED TO QUOTE
1) North American Rock    4)
2) Pratt & Whitney        5)
3) Beech Aircraft         6)
SELLER AWARDED PURCHASE ORDER
North American Rock

BUYER: North American Rock
CONTRACT NO. UR B(oo) B(00)
SUBJECT TO GOVERNMENT INSPECTION AT [X] YOUR PLANT [ ] GAEC [ ] NONE
PURCHASE ORDER NUMBER

CODE LR 5-
TELEPHONE-AREA CODE 516
CERTIFIED FOR NATIONAL DEFENSE USE UNDER DMS REG. I/SEE ARTICLE XII (D) ON BACK. / PRIORITY 1
DATE REC'D IN PURCH.
DATE RELEASED TO TYPE 4/13/70
FOB DESTINATION (UNLESS OTHERWISE INDICATED) Houston
TERMS Cash
DATE

| SHIP TO | | VIA | | |
|---|---|---|---|---|
| Hou-MSC | | LM-7, USS Iwo Jima, GOVAIR | | |

DELIVERY REQUIRED AT GAEC
DATE: None
QUAN.

SELLER PROMISE
Never Again

| ITEM NO. | QUANTITY | UNIT | PART NO. — DESCRIPTION | I-T | ACCT. NO./JOB NO. | TAX CODE | UNIT PRICE |
|---|---|---|---|---|---|---|---|
| 1. | 400,001 | Mi | Towing, $4.00 first mile, $1.00 each additional mile<br>Trouble call, fast service | | | | $ 400,004.00 |
| 2. | 1 | KWH | Battery Charge (road call + $.05 KWH)<br>customer's jumper cables | | | | 4.05 |
| 3. | 50# | # | Oxygen at $10.00/lb | | | | 500.00 |
| 4. | 1 | | Sleeping accommodations for 2, no TV, air-conditioned,<br>with radio, modified american plan, with view | | NAS-9-1100 | | Prepaid |
| 5. | | | Additional guest in room at $8.00/night  (1) Check out no<br>later than noon Fri. 4/17/70, accommodations not guaranteed beyond that time. | | | | 32.00 |
| 6. | | | Water | | | | No charge |
| 7. | | | Personalized "trip-tik", including all transfers,<br>baggage handling and gratuities | | | | No charge |
| | | | Sub-Total | | | | $ 400,540.05 |
| | | | 20% commercial discount + 2% cash discount (net 30 days) | | | (-) | 88,118.81 |
| | | | Total | | | | $ 312,421.24 |
| | | | No taxes applicable (government contract) | | | | |

SUGGESTED SOURCES/REMARKS (INCLUDE CWA NO. IF APPLICABLE):

RECEIVING DELIVER TO: USS Iwo Jima
VIA: Air Express
REQUESTED BY: NASA(MSC)    EXT.    PLT. & DEPT. NO.    DATE
APPROVED BY    DATE

GAEC
G 95 REV. 5 2-69 50M

ORIGINATOR

## APOLLO 13 TOWING INVOICE

Apollo 13 splashed down on April 17, 1970, with the safe recovery of the entire crew. The event is often referred to as the most successful "failed" mission in the space program. That same day, a tongue-in-cheek invoice for towing charges was delivered by Grumman to North American Rockwell (the manufacturer of the Apollo command module) listing $312,421.24, for the use of its lunar module in hauling the crippled spacecraft most of the way to the Moon and back. On receiving the bill, Earl Blount, a North American public-relations director, said, "Grumman, before sending such an invoice, should remember that North American Rockwell had not received payment for ferrying LMs on previous trips to the Moon."

**AMELIA EARHART RELICS** Amelia Earhart's place in American legend was secured in 1937. With navigator Fred Noonan, she took off from Miami, Florida, on June 1 in a Lockheed Electra, in an attempt to circle the globe. The pair flew over four continents and the South Atlantic. One month into the flight, they vanished while trying to reach Howland Island in the western Pacific Ocean. Coast Guard ships in the area heard her radio reports explaining that they were running low on fuel and needed navigational assistance, but no trace of them was ever found.

In early 1937, Earhart had frequented the Tribune Barber Shop in downtown Oakland, California. Before leaving for her around-the-world flight, she allegedly had her famous tousled locks cut there by her favorite barber, "Gus." After her disappearance, the shears were set aside.

The Lockheed Aircraft Corporation intended to present Earhart with a trophy had she completed her flight. It depicts the god Mercury holding a Lockheed Electra. In 1996, the National Aviation Club revived the trophy to honor the Stinson Sisters, Katherine and Marjorie, who taught flying in 1912 and trained pilots in World War I.

Both the scissors and trophy were collected by the Amelia Earhart American Legion Auxiliary Post No. 678 of Los Angeles and were presented as gifts to the Smithsonian Institution.

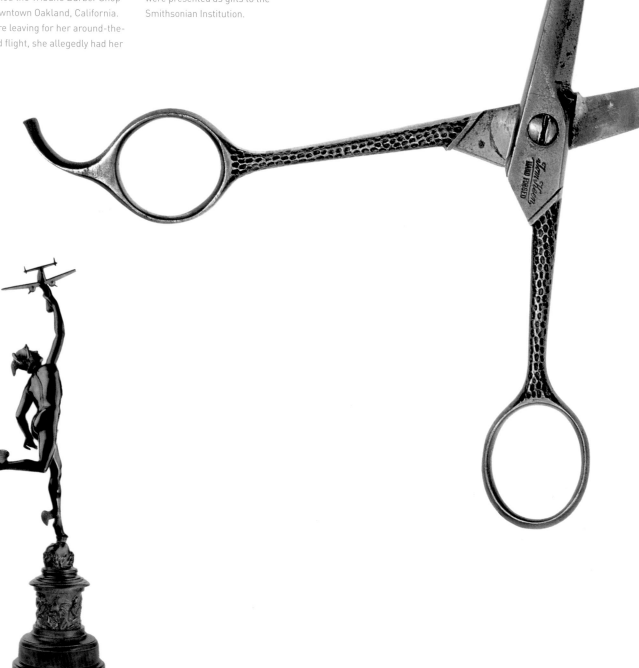

MY GVIDE FRIEND PROTECTOR

### ED WHITE'S RELIGIOUS MEDALS

Less than three months after the first spacewalk, by Soviet cosmonaut Aleksei Leonov on March 18, 1965, it was America's turn to take center stage in space. The performance lasted twenty-two minutes and was delivered by Gemini IV pilot Ed White on June 3, 1965; it was broadcast live and followed by millions over the radio and television sets.

Above the Indian Ocean in Earth orbit, White, tethered by umbilical hoses, slowly levitated from the hatch of the spacecraft. A burst from his "zip gun" released compressed nitrogen and propelled him away from the capsule and commander Jim McDivitt, who remained inside. White took photographs of Earth with a camera mounted on his spacesuit and told the world about the view and how great he was feeling. Floating freely, he accidentally bumped into the spacecraft, leaving a smudge on McDivitt's window. McDivitt remarked in jest, "You smeared up my windshield, you dirty dog. You see how it's all smeared up

there?" After about fifteen minutes, McDivitt asked Mission Control in Houston if there was anything they needed, and the response from Flight Controller Chris Kraft was, "Yes, tell him to get back in." White sighed and said, "It's the saddest moment of my life."

Ed White carried a number of personal items during his extra-vehicular activity, including three religious medals: a St. Christopher medal, a Crucifix, and a Star of David. A devout Methodist, White explained, "I had great faith in myself and especially in Jim, and also I think I had great faith in my God. So the reason I took those symbols was that I think this was the most important thing I had going for me, and I felt that while I couldn't take one for every religion in the country, I could take the three I was most familiar with." The Crucifix is reportedly somewhere inside the Gemini IV capsule in the *Milestones of Flight* gallery at the National Air and Space Museum. Ed White died on January 27, 1967, in the Apollo 1 fire.

### KATHRYN SULLIVAN'S GLOVES

Women first entered the realm of space when the Soviets launched twenty-three-year-old Valentina Tereshkova aboard Vostok 6 in 1963. The parachutist/assembly-line worker spent seventy hours in Earth orbit. Her flight, however, was an isolated event, as it would be almost twenty years before the Soviets put another woman into space — Svetlana Savitskaya, in 1982 — after NASA's selection of six female astronauts. Sally Ride became the first American woman astronaut in space, aboard the Space Shuttle *Challenger* in 1983. When the Soviets learned of NASA's plan to use astronaut Kathryn Sullivan for a future spacewalk, they again quickly launched Savitskaya, who in 1984 became the first woman to perform a spacewalk and the first woman to fly into space twice.

On October 5, 1984, NASA launched seven astronauts on board mission STS-41G, the largest crew ever. As part of the mission, Sullivan became the first American woman to walk in space,

when she and fellow astronaut David C. Leestma performed a 3½-hour extravehicular activity (EVA) on October 11. Their spacewalk demonstrated the feasibility of refueling satellites in orbit. The mission also included Sally Ride, on her second flight. It was the first mission to include two women crew members.

Although the flights of Tereshkova, Savitskaya, and Elena Kondakova in 1994 were both heroic and groundbreaking, they were the only women in the Soviet space program. Women have become fully integrated into the U.S. space program — and have excelled. For example, in 1996 astronaut Shannon Lucid set an American record after spending six months in space aboard the Russian Space Station *Mir*. In 1999 astronaut Eileen Collins commanded mission STS-93. The territory of space is embraced by all.

Kathryn Sullivan, a veteran of three missions, wore these gloves during her spacewalk in 1984.

**FIRST BUTTERFLIES IN SPACE** In 1999, high-school students from Albany, Georgia, designed a Space Shuttle experiment to determine how the lack of gravity would affect the metamorphosis of butterflies. They were participating in the S*T*A*R*S (Space Technology and Research Students) program started by SPACEHAB, a Houston, Texas–based company that provides commercial-payload processing services and laboratory facilities for NASA spacecraft. The goal of the program was to spark the imagination of high-school students and to encourage their interest in the field of microgravity research. As part of the experiment, butterfly larvae were flown on board STS-93 in a climate-controlled clear Lexan box. The cocoons hung from a bar inside the box, while a video system provided real-time imaging so that students worldwide could observe the insects via the Internet. Eventually these painted-lady butterflies (*Cynthia cardui*) emerged and fed on a mixture of leaves and grubs contained in the box.

In addition to the butterfly experiment, STS-93 deployed the Chandra X-Ray Observatory and also marked the first flight commanded by a woman, Lieutenant Colonel Eileen Collins.

**FIFTIETH ANNIVERSARY OF FLIGHT**
"Progress, Security" was the official motto for the fiftieth anniversary of powered flight. As this book goes to press, there are only a few months to go before the one hundredth anniversary of powered flight, December 17, 2003. How far has aviation progressed in the last fifty years? According to statistics from the U.S. Bureau of Transportation, more than 622 million people flew on American commercial airlines in 2001, compared to 35 million in 1954. In the last fifty years, the world has seen satellites orbiting the Earth in the 1950s, astronauts walking on the Moon in the 1960s, jumbo jets facilitating mass air transportation in the 1970s, routine Space Shuttle flights beginning in the 1980s, an armada of spacecraft exploring Mars in the 1990s, and men and women living and working on the International Space Station in the twenty-first century. The personal accomplishments of both men and women in the aviation and space field continue to encourage and inspire generations to come.

**CHILD-SIZED MERCURY SUIT** B.F. Goodrich, manufacturer of the spacesuits used for the Mercury space program, made a limited number of child-sized versions. These smaller suits were almost identical in appearance to the suits the Mercury astronauts wore on their flights. The gloves even included lights on the fingertips — a modification made after Alan Shepard's flight. The child-sized suits were used as gifts for VIPs. This is thought to be one of approximately six made by the company.

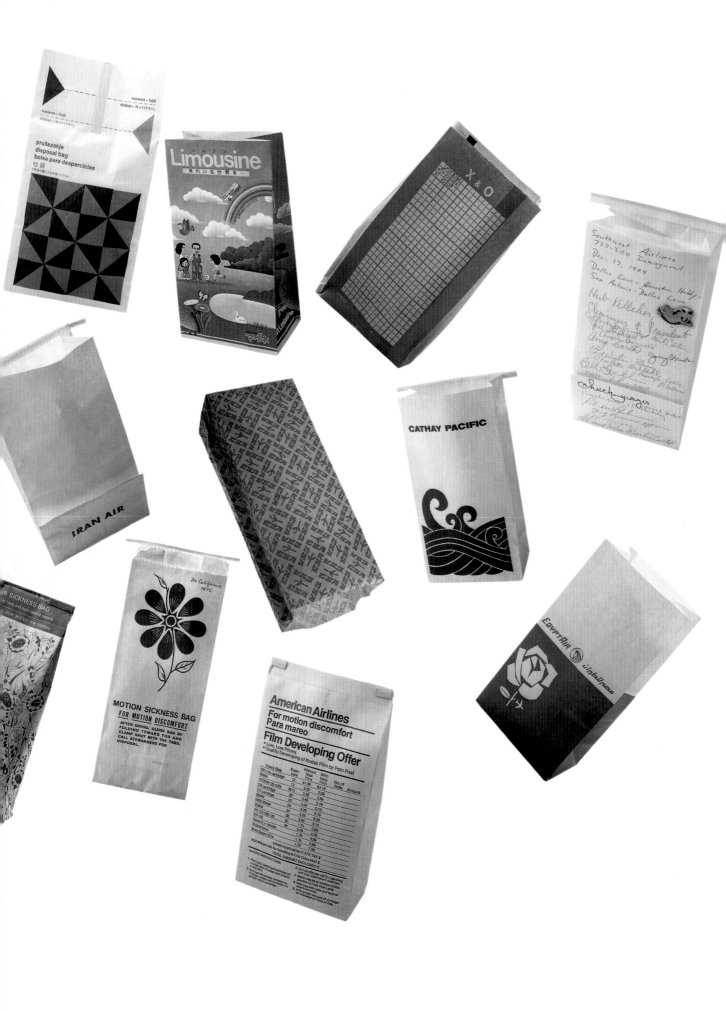

## MOTION-SICKNESS CONTAINERS

About one-third to one-half of all airline passengers will experience some amount of motion sickness when encountering severe turbulence. Symptoms generally consist of dizziness, fatigue, and nausea, which may progress to vomiting. Motion-sickness containers, better known as " barf bags," can be found on all major airliners to accommodate the weary traveler.

The National Air and Space Museum has a collection of more than 650 bags from airlines around the world. The bags, with their various designs, are all serviceable, but many of the airlines are now extinct.

**PLANE TICKETS** The first French commercial airline, the CMA (Compagnie des Messageries Aériennes), was founded in 1919 and reorganized as Air Union in 1923. The company's Paris-to-London route was a convenient option for travelers who otherwise would have to cross the English Channel by an overnight boat trip. The airline boasted of upholstered armchairs, large windows, radio-telephones, and newspapers on board their twin-engine cabin aircraft. Passengers were served a box lunch of sandwiches and a small bottle of white wine. Its motto was "Travel by air — safety, speed, pleasure, and comfort."

The fare between Paris and London was four hundred francs, which also included "free motor car conveyance for passengers and hand baggage from the center of the city to the air terminal." On each ticket Air Union printed its terms of liability, since regulations and laws had not yet been estab-lished for the commercial airline industry. It stated, "The Company and its Agents decline all respon-sibility relative to loss, or damage to passengers during their voyage, on the Company's machines owing to storms, fog, forced landings, strikes, leakages, fires, and all aerial disturbances either while rising, flying, or landing. . . . does not assume responsibility for the negligence or misconduct of its pilots or other employees or from any other cause." The airline transported 5,622 passengers in 1924, doubling its business from 1923, and commercial aviation was here to stay.

Air Union merged into Air France in 1933. In 1966, a spokes-person for Air France told the holder of the July 17, 1924, ticket seen here that it was the oldest known issued by the company.

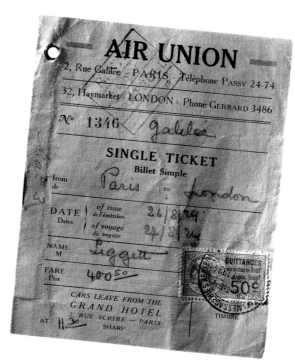

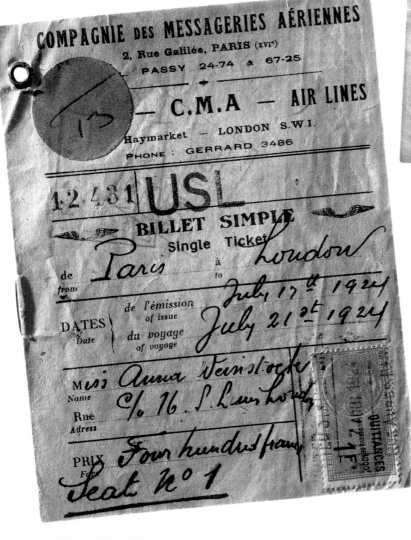

## TRAVELERS' INSURANCE MACHINE

For flying travelers, safety is always a concern. Even before the terrorist attacks of September 11, 2001, the commercial aviation industry was constantly scrutinized, monitored, and investigated. Although there are statistics to prove that air travel is the safest form of transportation, some passengers feel vulnerable despite the odds. According to the Bureau of Transportation Statistics, in the year 2000 more than 41,000 deaths were attributed to highway accidents as compared to 92 reported on American air carriers. By comparison, the number one killer in the United States is cardiovascular disease, with more than 875,000 deaths reported in 2000.

Having insurance is one way to relieve underlying fears or provide financial care for families and loved ones, on the off chance that an accident should occur. Up until the 1980s, insurance vending machines were available at most major airports. The machine could issue personal travel insurance in twenty-five-cent increments. Although insurance vending machines have mostly disappeared, one can still buy insurance at airport counters, travel agencies, or through the Internet.

This insurance vending machine was given to the museum when the Mercury International Company withdrew the last one from service.

**"HAP" ARNOLD'S STARS** General Henry H. "Hap" Arnold is considered the father of the U.S. Air Force. His personal contributions as an aviation pioneer and military leader led to its creation as a separate branch of America's military forces and to the growth of American airpower.

His military training began at West Point in 1904. After graduating in 1907 he was initially assigned to the infantry. Disgruntled, he was transferred to the aeronautical division of the Signal Corps, where he learned to fly, receiving the twenty-ninth pilot's license issued in the United States. During World War I, Arnold oversaw the Army's aviation training schools and engine manufacture, but his finest hours came later. On the eve of World War II, he maximized the Army Air Corps' readiness for combat with a civilian pilot training program. He contributed to the overall strategy of the war as a member of the Joint Chiefs of Staff and assisted in the organization of Allied control of the air in all theaters. In April 1944, he organized the 20th Air Force, a global strategic bombing force flying B-29s. In December 1944 he was promoted to the rank of five-star General of the Army.

After a career as an Army aviator and commander that spanned two world wars, he retired from active service in 1946. In May 1949 he was named General of the Air Force by President Harry S. Truman — the only officer to hold five-star rank in two military branches.

**SILENT PROPELLER** In 1946–47, research was undertaken by the National Advisory Committee for Aeronautics at the Langley Laboratory in Virginia to develop a "silent" propeller. The purpose was to reduce the noise generated by private aircraft in densely populated areas.

Experiments conducted in 1935 had determined that the noise level of an aircraft could be significantly reduced by using a propeller with a large blade area and low tip speed. This propeller is one of two built at Langley to these specifications. The wooden blades are each forty-two inches long, and the propeller has a total diameter of ninety-six inches. In tests on a Stinson L-5 airplane with a muffled 185-horsepower engine flying at 130 miles per hour at an altitude of three hundred feet, no distinct sound from the engine or propeller could be heard by a person on the ground. Although the effectiveness of the silent propeller was undeniable, it was too heavy for private aircraft and would have been too expensive to manufacture. Five-blade propellers were a rarity for that era. It was not until 1987 that modern technology allowed five-blade propellers to be manufactured effectively and inexpensively for commercial use.

**WILBUR WRIGHT'S LETTER** In 1899, a letter arrived at the Smithsonian Institution seeking information on the subject of aeronautics. The request came from a bicycle-shop owner named Wilbur Wright, in Dayton, Ohio. Restless with his current occupation, he and his brother had begun to pursue an alternative interest. Compiling information for their research, they eventually contacted the Smithsonian.

In his letter, dated May 30, Wilbur writes, "I have been interested in human flight ever since [I was] a boy....I wish to obtain such papers as the Smithsonian Institution has published on this subject, and if possible a list of other works in print in the English language....I am an enthusiast, but not a crank in the sense that I have some pet theories as to the proper construction of a flying machine...."

This was the first of several letters from the Wright brothers to the Smithsonian Institution. In June, the Assistant Secretary of the Smithsonian, Richard Rathbun, replied, "I am authorized to enclose herewith a list of works relating to aerial navigation... and under separate cover, several pamphlets bearing upon this subject which have been published by the Smithsonian Institution."

Wright's letter was accessioned as part of the collection of the National Air and Space Museum because of its subject matter. However, for conservation reasons, it was transferred to the Smithsonian Institution Archives, located in the Arts and Industries Building, only steps away from where it was originally received.

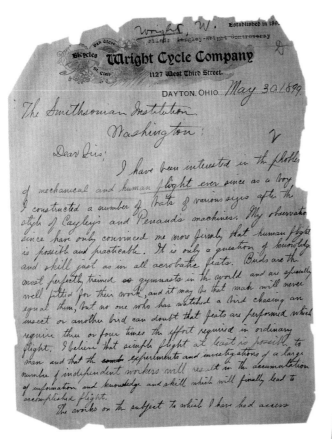

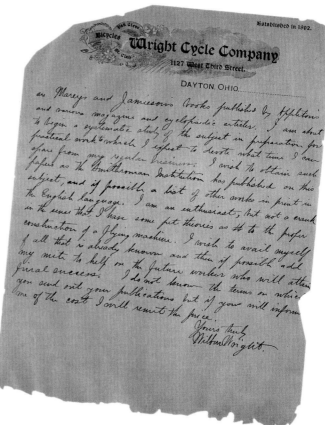

**CHARLES LINDBERGH'S CARIBBEAN MAP** After Charles Lindbergh's triumphant solo transatlantic flight, the "Lone Eagle" embarked on a tour sponsored by the Guggenheim Fund for the Promotion of Aeronautics. The journey began in July 1927 and covered 22,350 miles and forty-eight states. Lindbergh demonstrated the dependability of scheduled flying by keeping to an itinerary and landing in predetermined cities at precisely 2:00 P.M. each day. Along the route he made speeches, attended dinners and parades, and dropped messages from the air in cities where he was not scheduled to stop.

In December, he embarked on a Pan-American tour in the *Spirit of St. Louis*, with a nonstop flight from Washington, D.C., to Mexico. The tour continued across Central America, to Panama, Venezuela, back to Trinidad, across the Lesser Antilles, and through the West Indies. On February 8, 1928, Lindbergh made his last speech, in Havana, Cuba, before returning to the United States. On the completion of the tour, the *Spirit of St. Louis* was given to the Smithsonian Institution along with many items, including flight clothing, survival equipment, and maps.

This map of the Caribbean, carried by Lindbergh on the Pan-American tour, was exhibited in its original folded condition for several years. A new treasure was revealed to museum curators when the map was recently removed from display and unfolded. The back of the map is covered with Lindbergh's handwritten speech, which he penciled en route to Cuba while piloting the *Spirit of St. Louis*.

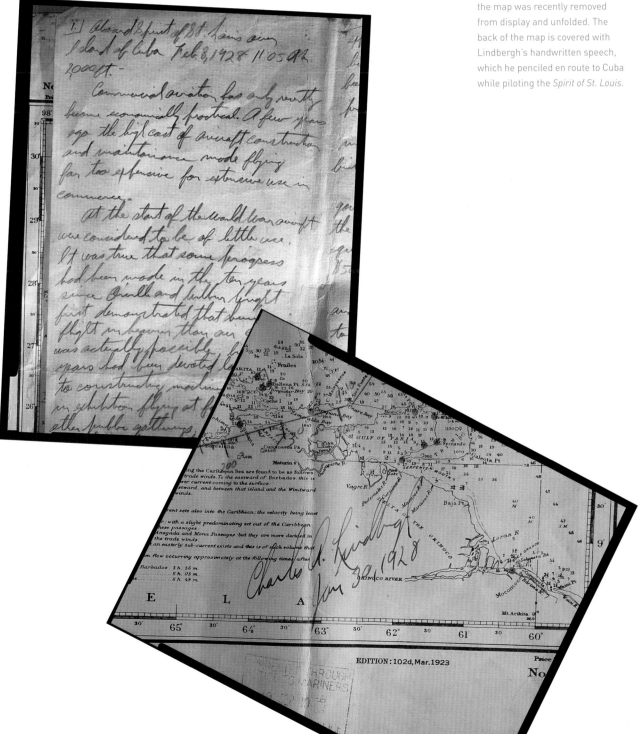

**WILLIAM BERTELSEN'S AERO-
MOBILE** Although Christopher
Cockerell is recognized as the inventor of the hovercraft in England
in the late 1950s, Dr. William R.
Bertelsen's earlier Aeromobile
35-A was probably the first hovercraft to carry a human over land
and water. Bertelsen invented his
drivable "air-cushion" vehicle as a
travel alternative to attend house
calls on snow-blocked roads in
rural Illinois. The basic principle of
the Aeromobile was a low-riding
sled design that glided on compressed air over land, water, snow,
or ice surfaces. Bertelsen began
with a vacuum-cleaner motor/fan
unit and progressed to a 72-horse-
power McCulloch 2-cycle, 4-cylinder
engine with an eight-blade wooden
propeller. The A-72 model was an
eight-by-five-foot structure built of
wood and aluminum, and in proper
conditions it could easily cruise at
60 miles per hour.

At one point Bertelsen's company sold Aeromobiles for $1,325,
as well as do-it-yourself plans,
with the following warning: "The
current design has no flotation
device and if the engine stops over
water it will sink to the bottom
unless a flotation device is added;
The operation of the Aeromobile
over dusty surfaces may result
in sand blasting nearby objects
and persons; The propeller fan is
near the top of the duct within
easy reach of hands." The doctor
attempted to market the Aeromobile in the medical field as a
supplement to the ambulance
and evacuation helicopter, but
without success.

He developed his Arcopter
series of ultralights in 1959, and
in 1975 he conceived of the innovative "Aeromobile–Aeroduct System":
"ground-effects machines" would
run on "aeroducts" located adjacent to highways or in storm drains.
Bertelsen believed this could provide mass transportation in rural
countries without rails or roads.
Now in his eighties, Bertelsen
continues to invent and promote
hovercraft technology with his
own company, Aeromobile, Inc.

**PRINCETON AIR RHO CAR** The Air Rho Car was a joint effort of Rhoades Inc., a Pennsylvania-based company, and Princeton University's Department of Aeronautical Engineering in the late 1950s and early 1960s. The vehicle is also referred to as the Princeton Air Scooter.

The Air Scooter was nine feet in diameter, had a bicycle seat and handlebars, and was powered by a Yamaha 250cc motorcycle engine. The propeller forced air through an outlet underneath the machine, which produced a cushion of air for the scooter to float on. The pilot steered by shifting his or her weight or by using the handlebars to direct the air through more than one hundred vents at various angles. It was reportedly the first foreign hovercraft to appear in England, the center of hovercraft innovation.

Princeton's interest in the project was to investigate the practicality of small ground-effect machines. In the late 1960s the university helped to design similar machines, such as the flying-saucer-shaped "Ag-gem," a hover-craft intended for the unlicensed crop-duster pilot.

**ROBERT GODDARD'S A-SERIES ROCKET** The pioneer of modern rocketry, Robert H. Goddard, had his first vision of spaceflight from the branches of a cherry tree. It was 1899 and he was seventeen. He wrote, "I imagined how wonderful it would be to make some device which had even the possibility of ascending to Mars, and how it would look on a small scale, if sent up from the meadow at my feet." Rockets at that time were used only for fireworks and signals, and it wasn't until 1909 that Goddard thought of them as a means to realize his dream. As a student at Worcester Polytechnic Institute in Massachusetts, he made and fired off rocket powder in the basement of the school, which brought him to the attention of the school's administrators. To their credit, he wasn't expelled. In 1915, Goddard's experiments became more systematic. Then, in 1921, he switched to liquid fuels. One of his greatest achievements was the world's first successful liquid-propelled rocket, launched March 16, 1926.

Goddard's A-Series rockets were tested in 1934–35, ascending more than a mile at speeds of up to 700 miles per hour. The nose cones concealed gyroscopic stabilizers that provided directional control. This particular rocket reportedly attempted a flight on September 23, 1935, with Goddard's benefactor Harry Guggenheim and supporter Charles Lindbergh present at the Roswell, New Mexico, launch site. (The Smithsonian Institution also provided funding for Goddard's early work.) A technical problem prevented a successful flight, but Lindbergh encouraged Goddard to document the progress by donating a rocket to the Smithsonian Institution. In November 1935 Goddard did so, with the following stipulation: "It is not desirable to have it on exhibition for a time, in order to give me the opportunity of completing the work to the extent of reaching an important height before details of construction are made public." Goddard died in 1945, and the rocket was displayed in 1951. This A-Series rocket, measuring approximately fifteen feet, is the earliest liquid-propellant rocket in the museum's collection.

**ASTRON SCOUT** As a direct response to the space race between the United States and the Soviet Union in the late 1950s, youngsters began experimenting with rockets that they built in their own basements and flew from their backyards. A successful launch — or failure — allowed them to experience the same emotions designers, engineers, and astronauts felt in real life. However, in those early days explosives were not regulated very well, and kids began hurting or even killing themselves with increasing frequency. A pipe from the hardware store, stuffed with match heads, might shoot several hundred feet into the air like a rocket. Just as easily it could also detonate, with catastrophic consequences.

The answer to safe rocketry came from a shoe salesman named Orville Carlisle, who was also an authority on fireworks. He was able to design a self-contained rocket engine that would fire only when ignited by a fuse. The same engine exploded a small charge once the rocket reached peak altitude, pushing a parachute out of one end of the rocket body and resulting in a safe landing. Carlisle, together with other rocket enthusiasts, including G. Harry Stine, founded Model Missiles of Denver, Colorado, which began selling safe rockets and engines through ads placed in magazines. Largely through Stine, model rocketry also became a regulated and safe hobby. The demand for his rockets was so popular that Model Missiles was overwhelmed and contracted with Estes Fireworks to build rocket engines.

Vern Estes put together a machine that could manufacture a reliable model-rocket engine every five and a half seconds. One of Estes' employees soon began calling the temperamental machine "Mabel" after an old love interest who had a similar personality. Mabel more than met Model Missiles' demand, and Estes was left with a surplus of model-rocket engines. As a result, he began producing his own model-rocket kits, beginning with the Astron Scout. When Model Missiles went out of business, Estes Industries was in position to become the world's leading model-rocket manufacturer. To date over 300 million model rockets have been launched, without a single accident.

Pictured here is one of the prototype Astron Scout kits that Estes gave to Stine to build and test. Recognizing its historical significance, Stine donated it to the Smithsonian in 1972, along with a sizable collection of other model-rocket artifacts. It is held by Vern Estes.

**SHEET MUSIC** The earliest known music with an aeronautical theme is the French song "Chanson sur le globe aerostatique," published in 1785 and referring to the first balloon ascensions in Paris. As paintings, drawings, jewelry, and decorative fabrications mirrored early aeronautical events, so did popular music.

During the 1920s, Bella C. Landauer, an avid collector of American advertisements (bookplates, liquor labels, lottery tickets, and funeral calling cards), also collected sheet music with an aeronautical theme. The earliest song in the Landauer collection is a German one, titled "The Goose, an Aviatrix," published by F.H. Himmel in 1802. The lyrics are about a gloating goose's superiority complex to the world below as she flies above Berlin. As soon as she lands, her ego is deflated once she realizes that she and her contemporaries are on equal ground. The moral: "No matter how high one gets in the world, it doesn't pay to become conceited."

Later songs celebrated aviation heroes, from the "Song of the Wright Boys" and "Come Josephine in My Flying Machine" to the most popular songs about Lindbergh. Personal and mechanical tragedies are represented in "The Hand of Fate," about the wreck of the *Shenandoah*, and "Amelia Earhart's Last Flight."

The sheet-music covers vividly illustrate balloons, flying machines, airplanes, airships, and famous flights. They preserve the essence of aviation history in words and pictures. There are more than 1,500 musical arrangements in both English and foreign languages in the Smithsonian Institution Library, National Air and Space Museum.

## WALLY SCHIRRA'S HARMONICA AND THOMAS STAFFORD'S JINGLE BELLS

The original goal of Gemini VI, crewed by Walter Schirra and Thomas Stafford, was to rendezvous with an unmanned Agena satellite. The launch, set for October 25, 1965, was scrubbed because the Agena blew up shortly after its launch. NASA went ahead with its flight schedule and soon launched Gemini VII. The Gemini VI mission was rescheduled to rendezvous with Gemini VII. This would be the first time two American spacecraft attempted a rendezvous in Earth orbit.

On December 15, 1965, Gemini VI met up with Gemini VII, and the two spacecraft flew in formation for about five hours. Then, suddenly, Thomas Stafford made an urgent radio transmission to Gemini VII and Mission Control in Houston, reporting a UFO.

"Houston, Gemini VII, this is Gemini VI. We have an object, looks like a satellite, going from north to south, probably in a polar orbit. He is in a very low trajectory, traveling from north to south, looks like he may be going to reenter very soon . . . stand by one — looks like he is trying to signal us."

The message was immediately followed by a rendition of "Jingle Bells" played on a tiny harmonica and a small string of bells. Thus, the spirit of the winter season was brought into the mission. The astronauts had prepared for their duet by attaching dental floss and Velcro to the instruments so they could be hung on the wall of the spacecraft when not in use. Schirra played a miniature Hohner harmonica, and Stafford backed him up on the bells. This was the first time musical instruments were played in space.

**GEMINI VII**  The Gemini missions trained astronauts and tested procedures in support of future Apollo missions to the Moon. Gemini VII, the fourth of ten manned Gemini launches, lasted fourteen days, December 4–18, 1965, setting a manned-spaceflight record that held until the flight of Skylab 2 in 1973. The mission was primarily an endurance test for astronauts Frank Borman and Jim Lovell. Medical experiments were conducted in the capsule to evaluate the effects of weightlessness and confinement on the crew. During launch, the astronauts wore specially designed lightweight spacesuits, which they eventually took off, thus becoming the first crew to work in a shirtsleeve environment while in space. For the first time, both crew members were also on the same sleep schedule. To pass the time, they brought books to read. Appropriately, Borman brought Mark Twain's *Roughing It*.

Although it wasn't in the plan, the mission participated in the first manned rendezvous in space. To maintain NASA's schedule, Gemini VII was launched before Gemini VI, which had experienced a launch failure, and it became the rendezvous target for the later mission. On December 15, "a wave of elation came over the Mission Control Center in Houston" when astronauts Wally Schirra and Tom Stafford on board Gemini VI reported that they were within 120 feet of the Gemini VII spacecraft. "Everyone in the Operations Room brought out a small American flag and fastened it to his console." The two spacecraft gradually drew within a foot of each other.

The splashdown of Gemini VII occurred within about 7.5 miles of its predetermined landing site, ending one of the most successful spaceflights in American history.

## JACK NORTHROP'S FLYING WING

Jack Northrop first envisioned an unconventional all-wing airplane design, without a fuselage or tail, in 1923. His design resulted in the X-216H two-seater aluminum-alloy "flying wing" built by the Avion Corporation in 1929. Although the plane fell short of a pure flying wing because of its external control surfaces and outrigger tail booms, it did pave the way for his later successes. With the establishment of his own company, Northrop Aircraft Inc., he was able to produce the N-1M Flying Wing in 1939–40.

The N-1M prototype had a wingspan of thirty-eight feet. It was constructed of wood and welded steel tubing so that changes could be made during the course of its development. Test pilot Vance Reese made the initial flight on July 3, 1940, and he reported that the plane could fly no higher than five feet off the ground. It went through a series of modifications, primarily to the wingtips and the "elevons," the trailing-edge controls. With an assortment of improvements and various test pilots at the controls, the N-1M flew more than two hundred successful flights. However, the overall flight performance of the plane was problematic. It was underpowered and overweight. Despite its flaws, Northrop persuaded General Henry "Hap" Arnold that the N-1M was adequate to serve as the template for more advanced flying-wing concepts. It was the forerunner of the N-9M and the larger and longer-range XB-35 and YB-49 flying wings.

In 1945, Northrop presented his N-1M to the Army Air Forces for the museum price of one dollar. The plane was given to the Smithsonian in 1946, and in 1983 it was restored to its original condition. It is one of only two surviving Northrop Flying Wings.

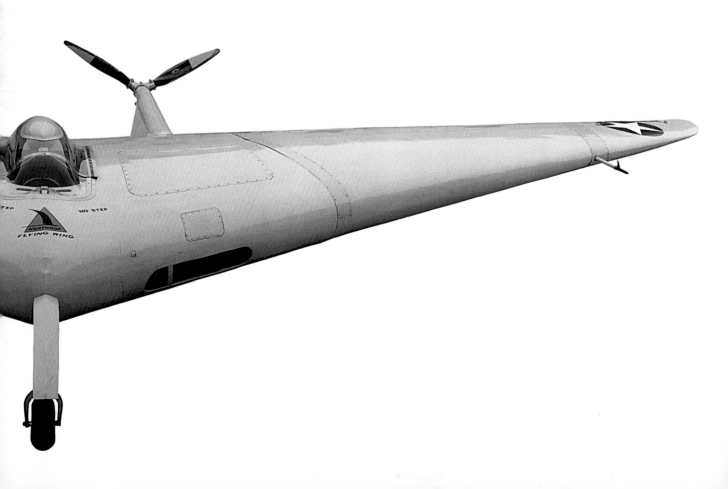

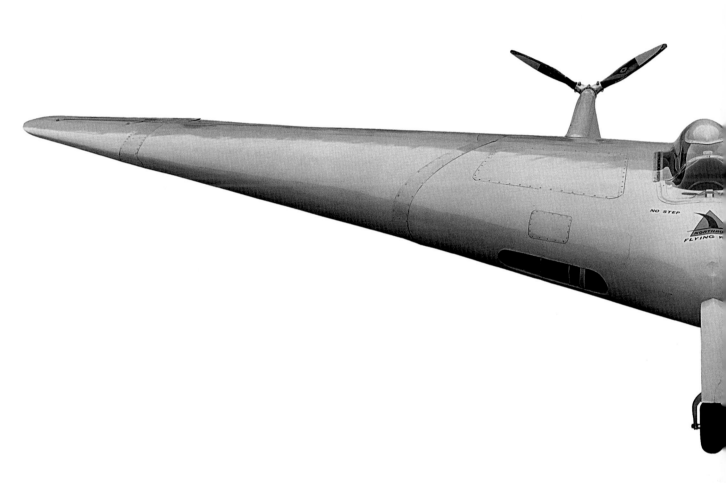

**SPACE AGE LUNCHBOX** Beginning in 1967, the Smithsonian staff held "lunchbox forums" where curators and special guests were invited to give informal talks about aviation and astronautics. The forums met originally in the Smithsonian Institution Arts and Industries Building, where the collection was then exhibited, and then later at the National Air and Space Museum after it was opened in 1976.

The forums began with the lecture "Statistical Survey of Features of Mars," by Carl Lineau. Other wide-ranging topics covered during these lunchtime briefings included "Aeronautics in 1870" by Ernst Cohen, "Early Ordnance of Rockets" by Frederick C. Durant, "Mapping of Mars" by James Edson, "Preliminary Scientific Results of the Lunar Landings" by Farouk El-Baz, "Soviet Space Program on the Tenth Anniversary of Sputnik" by Charles Sheldon, "Flying Is My Career" by Jacqueline Cochran, and "The Douglas World Cruisers" by Major General Leigh Wade.

This aluminum lunchbox made in 1960 beautifully demonstrates the influence of the Space Age on American popular culture. It also served as the symbol of the lunchbox forums, and, when placed in the center of the table, it signaled that the lecture was in progress. The lunchbox remained a welcome presence at the forums, which lasted until at least 1978.

## RX-1 EXPERIMENTAL HARD SUIT

Fashion conscious NASA was not, but with the goal of putting a man on the Moon, his wardrobe became a priority. During the Apollo program, many companies submitted designs to NASA for potential "Moon Wear." The RX suits were a series of experimental spacesuits developed by Litton Industries in the 1960s. The ensemble consisted of an aluminum-alloy hard-shell design, with stainless steel and brass fittings. The joints were made of a rubberized material, and the suit opened at the waist and closed with a special "dog lock" across the torso.

Weighing up to ninety pounds, the suits proved to be puncture- and tear-proof but failed to main-tain a constant volume while performing a full range of body movements. The RX suits were also too heavy and difficult to store in the tight space in the Apollo spacecraft. Although the Apollo astronauts did not wear these suits, the concept has not been forgotten. NASA is currently experimenting with a hard torso design to support spacewalks on the International Space Station.

The RX-1 prototype shown here is one of five RX suits designed by Litton Industries.

123-

**BRANIFF TIGHTS** The image of Braniff Airways went psychedelic in 1965, thanks to Mary Wells, the "little Blonde Bomber" of advertising. The Dallas-based airline was in the process of expanding its routes when Wells was hired to promote it. Using original art, fashion, and advertising, she reinvented the airline, evoking a fun, sexy, modern approach to air travel. At Love Field the terminals were redesigned with mirrors, mood lighting, and Op Art colors. The airplanes were painted by Alexander Calder, which spurred the company's campaign, "The End to a Plain Plane."

Next came the revamping of airline "hostess" uniforms, with fashions by Italian designer Emilio Pucci. Until then, airline attendants had worn military-style suits in drab hues of olive or navy blue, which had hardly changed since the 1930s. The new "chic feminine" wardrobe produced by Pucci, in his trademark colors of pink, absinthe green, bold blue, melon, and apricot, revolutionized the look of the airline attendant. The flying fashionistas, with their short dresses,

cropped jackets, turtlenecks, and wraparound skirts, became style leaders. Influenced by the Apollo flights, Pucci also made plastic bubble-shaped space hats, which kept hairdos neat and tidy.

Mary Wells's image campaign worked, and sales skyrocketed 41 percent and profits increased 114 percent in the first six months of 1966. The industry took note and soon other airlines were changing their uniforms, influenced by the Braniff "girls." Pucci designed his last collection for Braniff in 1974. After fifty-four years of service, the airline was shut down in 1982. As the 1980s brought about changes in the industry, new fashions, and sensitivity to gender issues, airline attendant uniforms have come full circle back to the more conservative styled suits of the 1930s and 1940s.

Braniff airline attendants wore these Pucci-designed diamond-patterned tights in 1966, with a matching mini-length tunic, and derby hat.

**OPIUM PIPES** Opium pipes are made of various materials, ranging from bamboo, shell, ivory, reptiles, and assorted woods, to porcelain and stones such as jade. These unusual opium pipes were accepted into the collection at the National Air and Space Museum because they are crafted from aircraft parts. The stems of the pipes appear to be airplane fuel lines. The pipes were made sometime during World War II in China, where the smoking of the poppy plant was prevalent.

A missionary living in China during the war brought these pipes back to the United States, along with other U.S. Army Air Forces souvenirs, including badges and pins.

**AVIATOR'S FACE MASK** In July 1918, the Smithsonian Institution requested from the War Department samples of armament, equipment, and clothing worn by World War I military aviators to create a new collection for an exhibition about the modern soldier.

One article of flight clothing issued to Army pilots and flight crews was a wool-lined leather winter face or flying mask. The mask protected aviators and crew from extreme climate conditions in exposed open cockpits.

With the increased use of the closed cockpit and the development of the modern oxygen mask in the 1930s, flying masks were used less often. However, masks made of chamois were issued to pilots in World War II for high-altitude, arctic, and other cold-weather operations.

**AVIATOR GOGGLES** An alternative to the flying mask worn by early aviators was the half-mask goggles. These fur-lined goggles with glass lenses were used with a winter helmet for protection in open-cockpit aircraft. British pilots in the Royal Flying Corps wore this type of goggles during World War I.

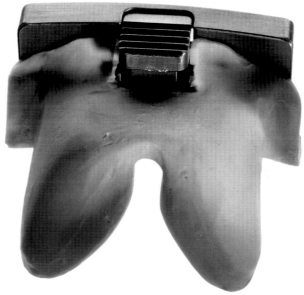

**VALSALVA DEVICE** Astronauts wear helmets for launch, spacewalks, and reentry. During extravehicular activities (EVAs), their helmets often are on for hours at a time, sealed and locked onto their suits. Have you ever wondered how they can scratch an annoying itch under their helmets?

Attached to the interior of the EVA helmet, there is a rubber V-shaped gadget called a Valsalva device. It was created to relieve ear pressure or earaches, which normally occur with changes of air pressure in the cabin. When the nose is placed inside the Valsalva device and blown, it clears the Eustachian tubes, thus relieving the pressure built up in the middle ear. Astronauts reported the device was seldom used for ear pressure, but it works great for pesky nose itches. It is often referred to as the helmet nose scratcher.

This Valsalva device was flown on Skylab 3.

## GEORGE WASHINGTON'S LETTER

With the ascent of the *Globe* and *Montgolfier* in 1783, the citizens of Paris witnessed the world's first balloon flights. Among the people in Paris were Benjamin Franklin, Thomas Jefferson, and John Quincy Adams. A young Philadelphia surgeon named John Foulke, also in France and a friend of Franklin's, became fascinated with the latest phenomenon.

On his return to Philadelphia, Foulke made demonstrations of paper hot-air balloons that rose to "perhaps three times the height of the houses and then gently descended without damage." He also arranged a lecture on ballooning at the University of Pennsylvania. Foulke sold tickets to his lecture and passed out complimentary invitations to individuals of social importance, including General George Washington. With regret, Washington declined, pleading prior commitments.

The letter says, "Genl. Washington presents his compliments to Doctr. Foulke — thanks him for his polite card and ticket — and

would with great pleasure attend his Lecture on Pneumatics, but the business which brought him to the city does not leave him at liberty, as the Members of the Cincinnati are anxious to bring it to a close. Monday Morning." Attached to the note was the returned ticket. A month after Foulke's lecture, a thirteen-year-old boy named Edward Warren, from Baltimore, Maryland, became the first American to ascend on a tethered balloon flight, on June 24, 1784.

Although Washington did not attend the lecture, as president he not only viewed but also assisted with the balloon ascent of the famous Jean-Pierre Blanchard on January 9, 1793. With a final salute by his artillery before Blanchard climbed in, one could say Washington gave his endorsement.

## JOHN STEINER'S BALLOON

German-born John Steiner made his mark on American soil by attempting to fly a balloon from Pennsylvania to Canada. On a June day in 1857, Steiner unwisely cast off from Erie in unfavorable weather conditions. With ominous storms approaching, he sailed over Lake Erie and into deafening thunder and bolts of lightning. On his approach to the Canadian shore near Long Point, the wind changed direction and blew him back over the lake toward Buffalo, New York. With the onset of night, Steiner realized that he would have to set down. He tried to land on the lake near the ship *Mary Stewart,* but every time he set down the balloon bounced back up twenty feet into the air. Eventually he jumped out and swam to the vessel. With a lost balloon and a defeated spirit, he returned home. In the end, the determined balloon made its lonely way to Canada. It was later found one hundred miles inland.

Despite the mishap, Steiner's career flourished, and he made numerous successful ascensions, serving in the Civil War as a balloonist for the Union forces, as a member of Thaddeus S.C. Lowe's Balloon Corps. In 1863, he gave a young Ferdinand von Zeppelin a tethered balloon ride in St. Paul, Minnesota. Steiner recounted the story of the runaway balloon and shared his ideas for new, improved balloons. It was to that chance meeting that Zeppelin attributed the conception of his "rigid" airships.

This ambrotype documents the inflation of John Steiner's balloon in Erie, Pennsylvania, on the day he departed for Canada, June 18, 1857. It is the oldest known photograph of ballooning in America. The photographer is unknown.

**SATURN V** The Saturn V was the largest interplanetary spaceship ever built. It was more than 363 feet tall and weighed more than 6 million pounds. It was capable of sending a 285,000-pound payload into Earth orbit or 100,000 pounds to the Moon. Thirteen of these massive rockets were launched between November 1967 and May 1973. Remarkably, all of them flew successfully, sending nine separate crews all the way to the Moon and back.

The first stage of the Saturn V was powered by five F-1 engines that produced more than 1.5 million pounds of thrust each. Like everything else about the Saturn V, the F-1s were gargantuan: the largest single-chamber thrust engines ever built. During launch, they produced a tremor that could be detected on seismographs 1,500 miles away.

Sadly, only three Saturn Vs remain. Although these rockets are displayed at NASA centers in Florida, Houston, and Alabama, all of them are, in fact, Smithsonian artifacts on loan. The stages composing the Saturn V at NASA's Kennedy Space Center in Florida come from surplus hardware, including the first stage (or S-IC stage) shown here. Originally it was used as part of the Interim Facilities Test Vehicle, which is better known as Saturn Apollo 500-F. This rocket was never intended to fly, but rather it allowed engineers at Kennedy Space Center to practice assembling flight-qualified hardware and to test the difficult process of transporting the Saturn V to the launch pad. The most noticeable difference is that the 500-F first stage had a different paint pattern from those of other Saturn Vs. Workers found that the black roll pattern on the first stage caused internal temperatures to be too high, so flight-qualified Saturn Vs were changed.

This Saturn was displayed outside the Vertical Assembly Building at Kennedy Space Center for nearly twenty years. During the 1990s it underwent a restoration and was repainted to match the markings on the Apollo 11 launch vehicle. It is now exhibited in its own building at the center.

**GUS GRISSOM'S GLOVES** Virgil Ivan "Gus" Grissom became the second American to launch into space, on June 21, 1961. Although his flight plan was similar to that of Alan Shepard's earlier flight, his spacecraft, *Liberty Bell 7*, included an overhead trapezoidal window for observations and was equipped for additional flight maneuvers. The flight lasted fifteen minutes, with splashdown occurring off the coast of the Bahamas. The hatch blew while Grissom was waiting for the recovery crew, and although he escaped from the water-filled capsule, the spacecraft was too heavy for the recovery helicopter and it sank to the bottom of the ocean. Without a life vest, Grissom nearly drowned, as his spacesuit also began to take in water. The incident resulted in a number of procedural and safety changes, including the addition of a mini–life vest to all astronaut survival kits.

Four years later, on March 23, 1965, Grissom became the first man to fly in space twice, as commander of the Gemini 3 mission. With the loss of *Liberty Bell 7* in mind, Grissom named his Gemini capsule *Molly Brown*, after the "Unsinkable" Molly Brown who survived the sinking of the *Titanic*. At one point in the flight, pilot John Young, who was responsible for experiments with new dehydrated space foods, asked Grissom, "Would you care for a corned beef sandwich, skipper?" Young had managed to sneak Grissom's favorite deli sandwich on board. After a successful mission, the *Molly Brown* lived up to her name and didn't sink. The five-hour flight was another step toward putting a man on the Moon.

Grissom was assigned to command the first Apollo flight in March 1966. Together with crew members Ed White and Roger Chaffee, he perished in a fire during a launch-pad test. They were the first casualties experienced by the U.S. space program as part of a mission.

Gus Grissom wore these gloves during training for his Mercury flight.

**SAFETY POSTER** After the success of the Mercury and Gemini space programs, the United States began final preparations for putting a man on the Moon. The first manned Apollo launch was scheduled for February 21, 1967. On January 27, 1967, a crew entered Command Module 012, which was sitting on top of the unfueled AS-204 rocket at Pad 34A, to practice launch procedures. Gus Grissom, Ed White, and Roger Chaffee were immersed in a pure oxygen environment for five hours as they encountered many wearisome test failures and repairs. Suddenly, catastrophe struck when a spark inside the oxygen-saturated cabin instantly ignited a flash fire. The capsule became a death trap, as the astronauts were unable to open a poorly designed hatch in time to save themselves.

The Apollo 204 accident review board stated that conditions at the time of the accident were "extremely hazardous." However, the simulated launch procedure exercise was not considered to be particularly dangerous by either NASA or the contractor prior to the accident. Consequently, adequate safety precautions were neither established nor observed. The amount and location of combustibles in the command module were not closely restricted and controlled, and there was no way for the crew to escape rapidly from the command module during this type of emergency — nor had procedures been established for ground-support personnel outside the spacecraft to assist the crew. The report led to major design and engineering modifications to the spacecraft, revisions in test planning and discipline, and changes in quality and safety control.

This safety poster, which depicts the doomed crew, was probably produced in late 1966 in a limited quantity. Years later it was pulled from a recycling bin at Cape Canaveral and sent to the museum.

## BILLY MITCHELL'S TRICYCLE

Following World War I, many Air Service pilots backed the idea of a new branch of the military separate from the Army or Navy that could carry out strategic air operations against enemy targets, rather than simply supporting frontline troops on the battlefield. The most outspoken advocate of this idea was Billy Mitchell.

In 1921, by conducting a series of tests off the coast of Virginia, Mitchell proved his theory that airpower could defend the nation's shorelines from enemy attacks. Mitchell's bombers sank three captured German naval vessels and the obsolete USS *Alabama*. Two years later, additional bombings were conducted, sinking other obsolete battleships. The results of the bombing tests encouraged the supporters of a separate air arm to push even further for their beliefs, but the Army General Staff remained firm in its notion that airpower could not win a war.

Mitchell became progressively more defiant of his superiors, until his bold public outbursts were no longer tolerable. He was suspended from duty for five years in December 1925 after being court-martialed for insubordination, under the all-inclusive 96th Article of War. The following year, Mitchell resigned from the service.

He died in 1936 and never saw his ideas come to fruition with the deployment of the Boeing B-17, the world's first long-range, high-altitude strategic bomber, in World War II. In 1946, however, Mitchell was posthumously awarded a Congressional Medal of Honor recognizing him for his foresight in American military aviation.

General Billy Mitchell is said to have made this pedal plane of wood and metal for his son at the family farm, Boxwood, in Middleburg, Virginia. In 1935, a year before Mitchell died, he gave the craft to fellow aviator and friend Carl Harper for his infant son, Bud Harper, who later donated it to the museum.

**GOOD-LUCK CHARM** Russian-born Paul Studenski held a law degree from the University of St. Petersburg and had finished a year of medical school at the Sorbonne in Paris when Louis Blériot flew the English Channel in 1909. Enthralled by the spectacle, the twenty-two-year-old put his academic plans on hold to learn how to fly.

He first soloed on November 8, 1910, and received the 292nd license issued by the Aéro-Club de France. Emigrating to America a year later, he worked as an instructor, test pilot, barnstormer, and exhibition flier. After only four short years of what could have been a lifetime of aviation, Studenski retired from the sky at the request of his wife. He went on to become a distinguished academic and died while browsing in a bookstore on November 2, 1961.

He carried this burlap doll as a good-luck charm on his flights.

**BLACKBIRD** With the maturing of the Cold War, the U.S. military asked for a reconnaissance aircraft that could fly deep within enemy territory without being intercepted by surface-to-air missiles. The answer came with the clandestine technology of the SR-71, or Blackbird. The SR-71 was designed to elude radar, fly at bullet speeds, and soar at altitudes so high that it was gone from enemy territory before it was even noticed.

The aircraft was almost ten years in the making. Conceptual development began at Lockheed's covert Skunk Works, headed by Clarence L. "Kelly" Johnson, in the late 1950s. Manufacturing and testing of the actual plane dated from February 1963, and its first operational sortie was flown over North Vietnam on March 21, 1968.

Its unusual shape is completely functional. The airframe was designed to reduce the reflection of radar, while the special black paint actually absorbed radar energy. As early examples of what is now known as "stealth" technology, these characteristics made the SR-71 difficult to detect. At operational speeds above Mach 3, atmospheric friction would cause conventional aluminum airframes to melt, so special titanium alloys were used. Outer surfaces were designed to accommodate heat expansion while in flight. The aerodynamic design of the aircraft consisted of "all-moving" control surfaces.

The bulk of the "spy" equipment was stored in the nose of the aircraft. The all-weather day-and-night Lockheed Martin ASARS-1 Advanced Synthetic Aperture Radar System, along with other sensors, could survey 100,000 square miles per hour. The data gathered by the ASARS was downloaded to ground intelligence stations via a common data link (CDL) with a range of more than 300 nautical miles.

The SR-71 was capable of reaching speeds of over 2,200 miles per hour and an altitude of 85,000 feet. Two Pratt & Whitney J-58 Ramjet engines, which delivered

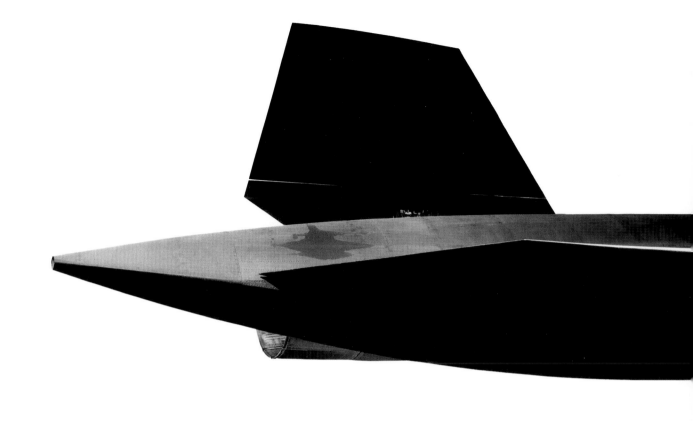

optimal performance and fuel efficiency at the highest speeds, powered the plane. The afterburners generated 32,500 pounds of thrust, sending a stream of shock diamonds through the sky. The exhaust nozzles glowed flaming red from the scorching temperatures of the afterburners. These nozzles emitted a characteristic green flame during takeoff, on account of the presence of tetra-ethyl borane in the fuel mixture. At higher speeds, the SR-71 used a special fuel with a high flash point called JP-7, which was difficult to ignite. The aircraft was capable of carrying 84,000 pounds of fuel and could be refueled in flight through a receptacle on top of the fuselage.

Each engine's air intake contained a circular center body with a cone-shaped "spike" at the tip. The spike controlled airflow into the engine, and it moved forward during takeoff and climbs and rearward during high-speed flight. As the air passed over the spike, the "air inlet bypass doors" inside the engine nacelle regulated the correct airflow through the engine, holding the supersonic shock wave in the critical position within the inlet. A condition referred to as "unstart" occurred when shock waves were expelled from the inlet. If unmonitored, the aircraft could yaw violently enough to shake up the aircrew. Fortunately, an automatic control could predict the problem and reposition the spike in milliseconds.

On March 6, 1990, Lockheed SR-71 Blackbird #972 set a new transcontinental speed record, going from coast to coast in slightly less than sixty-eight minutes on its final flight, after which it was retired to the National Air and Space Museum. A total of 389 people had the privilege and thrill of flying beyond Mach 3 in the Blackbird. One of them was the museum's Chief of Collections Management, Tom Alison, who flew #972 on more than a dozen operational sorties during his active Air Force service.

**_NORGE_ FOOD RATION**  On December 14, 1911, Norwegian-born Roald Amundsen became the first person to reach the South Pole, traveling by ship and dogsled. After several failed attempts to reach the North Pole by ship and airplane, the veteran explorer resorted to airship. To fund this new expedition, he approached the Italian government. The Italian leader, Benito Mussolini, provided a 670,980-cubic-foot semirigid N.1 airship, built by Umberto Nobile; Nobile himself to command it; and five crew members. The airship was refurbished and renamed the _Norge_.

With Amundsen's American friend Lincoln Ellsworth; pilot Hjalmar Riiser-Larsen, who served as navigator; and a dozen additional crew members, the _Norge_ set off from Spitsbergen, Norway, on May 11, 1926. The following day, after sixteen hours in the air, a triumphant crew dropped the Norwegian, American, and Italian flags over the North Pole.

On May 14, as the _Norge_ headed toward Nome, Alaska (the flight had been dubbed "Rome to Nome"), the airship encountered dreadful weather conditions. The crew set it down near Teller, Alaska, and the balloon was completely deflated. They had covered 3,400 miles in seventy-two hours, floating over uncharted polar territory and filling a gap on the world map. The flight gave Amundsen the distinction of being the first person to reach the Earth's two poles. (The North Pole had already been claimed by Robert Peary in April 1909.)

The love of Amundsen's life was Arctic exploration, but in the end it killed him. Two years after the flight of the _Norge_, Nobile attempted a second Arctic flight in the _Italia_. When his airship disappeared, Amundsen joined a search party to find him. Although another search team found Nobile, Amundsen and his crewmates never returned.

During Amundsen's stay in Teller, Alaska, while the _Norge_ was dismantled, he presented a helpful trader with a few souvenirs, including a can of food from the trip, which eventually made its way into the museum's collection.

**MEAL, READY-TO-EAT** The United States has delivered more than 10 million Humanitarian Daily Rations (HDR) to twenty-two countries around the globe. The original requirement for the HDR was based on a need identified by the Department of Defense to feed and sustain large populations of displaced persons or refugees under emergency conditions. The HDR is packaged in materials similar to the Meal, Ready-to-Eat (MRE) used by U.S. military personnel, but in keeping with cultural sensitivities the HDR is vegetarian. Each ration pack contains food equivalent to 2,200 calories and provides an entire day's nutritional requirement for one person: two main vegetarian meals based heavily on lentils, beans, and rice, but including items such as bread,

a fruit bar, a fortified biscuit, peanut butter, and spices.

This is an example of an HDR dropped over Afghanistan by the U.S. Air Force and U.S. Army Humanitarian Relief effort during Operation Enduring Freedom, following the terrorist attacks on the United States on September 11, 2001. These HDRs were unloaded from airborne C-17 aircraft using the Tri-Wall Air Delivery System, or TRIAD — specially designed containers. After a C-17 was depressurized over the drop zone, its cargo doors opened and the pilot would pull the aircraft's nose up about seven degrees. The loadmaster would then release the TRIADs, which were tied to static lines that tightened and then flipped the containers over once they were clear of the aircraft. The TRIADs would then open, disbursing the prepackaged food rations over the drop zone. The entire off-loading sequence takes about six seconds. C-17 aircraft distributed more than 2.5 million HDRs over Afghanistan.

The United States usually keeps about 2 million of the ration packs stockpiled for worldwide emergencies. The shelf life of the HDR is thirty-six months at 80 degrees Fahrenheit, and each ration packet costs about four dollars.

139—

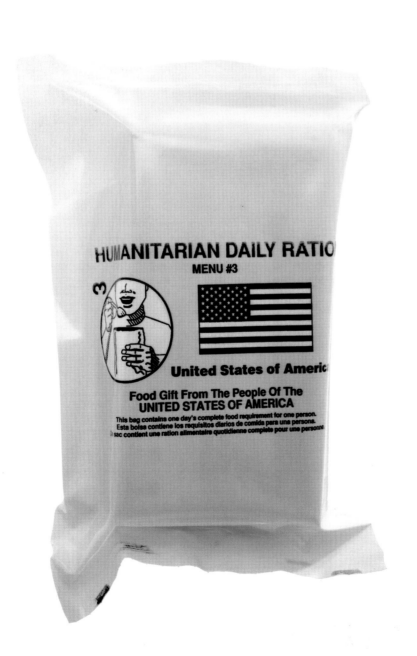

**FALLEN ASTRONAUT** "If we die, we want people to accept it. We're in a risky business, and we hope that if anything happens to us it will not delay the program. The conquest of space is worth the risk of life." — Gus Grissom, quoted in John Barbour, *Footprints on the Moon*

On Apollo 15, the fourth mission to land on the Moon, astronauts David Scott and James Irwin left a memorial on the lunar surface as a tribute to the heroic men of the U.S. and Soviet space programs who had risked and lost their lives. As the final act of the third extravehicular activity on August 2, 1971, they placed a sculpture depicting a "fallen astronaut" in the lunar soil at the Hadley-Apennine landing site. Next to it was a plaque listing the names of the deceased, in alphabetical order: Charles Bassett, Pavel Belyayev, Roger Chaffee, Georgi Dobrovolsky, Theodore Freeman, Yuri Gagarin, Edward Givens, Virgil Grissom, Vladimir Komarov, Viktor Patsayev, Elliot See, Vladislav Volkov, Edward White, and Clifton Curtis Williams Jr.

Paul Van Hoeydonck of Antwerp, Belgium, created the 3½-inch aluminum *Fallen Astronaut*, as well as this replica, identical to the one left on the Moon.

### SOLID ROCKET MOTOR O-RING
**HEATER** The Space Shuttle *Challenger* was NASA's second orbiter to become operational, and it flew a total of nine successful missions. However, on January 28, 1986, the STS-51L *Challenger* mission was lost seventy-three seconds after launch, when a booster failure resulted in the catastrophic breakup of the vehicle. All of the seven-member crew perished: Francis R. Scobee, Michael J. Smith, Judith A. Resnik, Ellison S. Onizuka, Ronald E. McNair, Gregory B. Jarvis, and Sharon Christa McAuliffe.

Analyses of photographic data revealed that a large cloud of gray smoke appeared in the vicinity of the aft field joint on the right solid rocket booster (SRB) shortly before liftoff. Investigators determined that low overnight temperatures had caused a rubber joint seal, or O-ring, to shrink. When the SRBs were ignited at launch, hot propellant gases were able

to burn through grease and joint insulation and compromise one of the seals. As the flight progressed, hot gases continued to burn through the broken seal, eventually destroying one of the attachment points between the right booster and the large external fuel tank. Because the booster was still firing, its nose was forced into the external tanks, releasing liquid oxygen and hydrogen in a massive explosion.

To prevent such a calamitous accident from happening again, Tayco Engineering developed the solid rocket motor (SRM) O-ring heater. This 40-foot-long, 1½-inch-diameter flexible heater maintains the temperature of the field joints at 75 degrees and protects them from freezing and cracking during launch preparations in cold-weather conditions. Since installing these devices, Space Shuttles have flown more than one hundred missions.

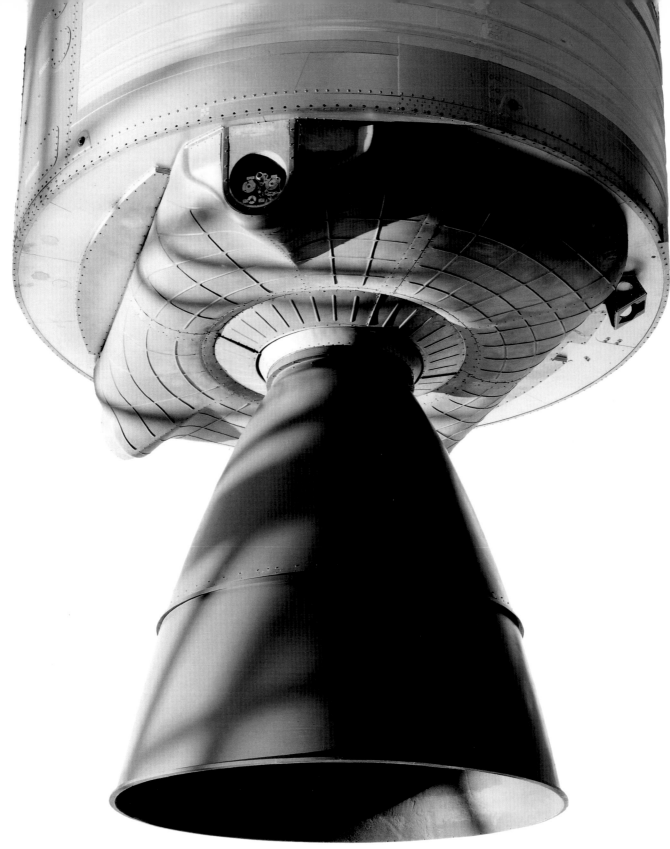

**APOLLO-SOYUZ MISSION** In July 1975, the Soviet Union and the United States participated in the first international joint venture in space. The Apollo-Soyuz Test Project was designed to test the compatibility of rendezvous and docking systems on American and Soviet spacecraft. The two manned spacecraft launched from their respective countries, rendezvoused, and then docked while in Earth orbit. The mission symbolized a period of reduced tension between two rival nations during the Cold War.

The spacecraft remained docked for a period of two days, during which time American astronauts Thomas Stafford, Vance D. Brand, and Donald K. Slayton and Soviet cosmonauts Aleksei Arkhipovich Leonov and Valeri Kubasov visited, shared meals, and worked on various tasks together in space.

On Earth, the United States and Soviet Union also partnered to celebrate the historic event. Among a number of commemorative items that were manufactured, Apollo-Soyuz cigarettes were produced by the American cigarette company Philip Morris and the Soviet Yava cigarette factory.

Before the mission could proceed, both countries had to reconcile differences in measuring systems, spacecraft, and adapter designs, and in air pressures and mixtures. A docking module, which enabled the two spacecraft to link in space, was designed and contracted to North American Rockwell by NASA. It served as an airlock and transfer corridor between the two spacecraft, since they had different atmospheres.

Shown is the service propulsion system of the Apollo Command Service Module, one of the most spectacular components of the American portion of the ASTP. It was originally used by NASA for vibration and acoustic tests in 1973.

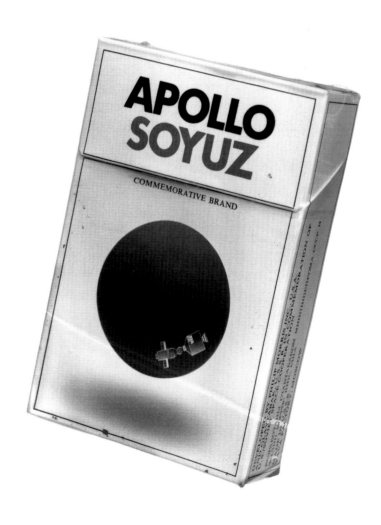

**PROPELLER FRAGMENT** Two years after the Wright brothers' first successful flights in 1903, they constructed their third flyer. This was the world's first practical powered airplane, capable of performing banking maneuvers, circles, and figure eights. On September 3, 1908, the new flyer based on the 1905 design was delivered to the drill grounds at Fort Myers, Virginia, for flight trials. If the aircraft met certain performance specifications, the U.S. Army would be obliged to buy it.

After several days of successful flights . . . catastrophe. On September 17, at 5:14 P.M., Orville Wright took off with a passenger, Lieutenant Thomas O. Selfridge. The aircraft had circled the field four and one-half times when the propeller blade split. The aircraft safely glided from 150 feet to 75 feet before stalling. It then pitched into the ground and shattered to pieces in front of 2,500 horrified spectators. Both men were thrown from the aircraft. Orville was hospitalized for six weeks with a broken thigh, three broken ribs, and other injuries. Selfridge suffered a fracture at the base of the skull and died later that evening. He became the first casualty of powered flight.

The Wrights completed the trials with a new airplane in 1909, which the Army purchased for $30,000. This propeller fragment from the 1908 crash appears with an original tag stating its authenticity.

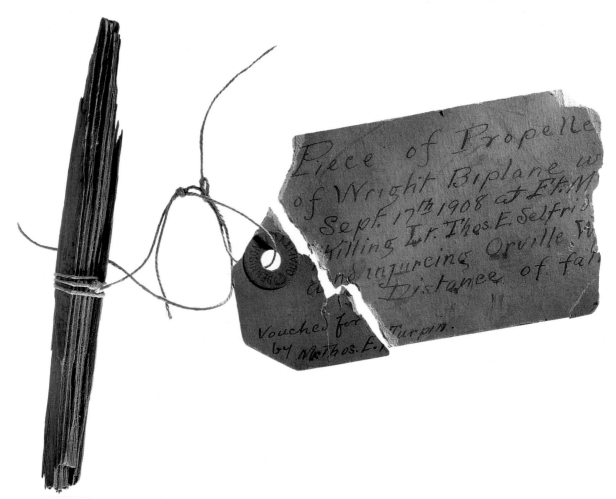

*Piece of Propelle of Wright Biplane w Sept 17th 1908 at Ft-M killing Lt. Thos. E Selfri and injuring Orville W Distance of fal*

*Vouched for by MrThos. E.* Turpin.

**KARA HULTGREEN'S FLIGHT JACKET**
In 1994, the Department of Defense rescinded the Risk Rule that banned women from becoming military combat pilots. This allowed Kara Hultgreen to become the U.S. Navy's first fully qualified female F-14 Tomcat pilot, after she successfully landed on the USS *Constellation* in the summer of 1994.

A few months later, while on a routine flight, her F-14 plane crashed during final approach to the deck of the USS *Abraham Lincoln,* off the coast of San Diego. Her radar intercept officer, Lieutenant Matthew Klemish, was able to eject safely and was rescued. However, the plane was rolling, and when Hultgreen ejected she was pointing down toward the ocean. Reportedly her body was found, nineteen days later, still strapped to the ejection seat and wearing this jacket.

Controversy surrounded the accident. Questions were raised regarding Hultgreen's flight record, and some suggested that the Navy had rushed to integrate women into the ranks and placed an unqualified person in the cockpit. After a four-month investigation, it was determined that pilot error was not the cause of the crash. Hultgreen's flight records were also made public, and they documented her competence, such as the fact that she had graduated third of seven in her pilot-training class. Hultgreen was buried with military honors at Arlington National Cemetery.

## CUBAN MISSILE CRISIS MODEL

Early in 1962, U.S. intelligence sources reported increased Soviet movements in Cuba, arousing suspicion that they were building a military base. On October 14, 1962, U-2 reconnaissance aircraft flew over Cuba and brought back photographs revealing that medium-range ballistic missiles were being installed in San Cristóbal. Faced with the serious threat of a missile strike, the U.S. armed forces were placed at their highest state of alert.

After a tense thirteen-day standoff between President John F. Kennedy and Premier Nikita Khrushchev, the Soviet missiles were removed from Cuba on the (unpublicized) condition that the United States remove its missiles stationed in Turkey.

This SA-2 Launch Site model, based on images obtained from U.S. Air Force reconnaissance flights over Cuba, was constructed by the National Photographic Interpretation Center and was used in briefings with President Kennedy during the crisis. The photographs, made with a KA-18A Stereo Strip Camera, were taken by pilots flying U-2 and RF-101 aircraft sometimes as low as five hundred feet. U-2 pilot Major Rudolf Anderson lost his life when he was shot down during a reconnaissance mission.

**FRANCIS GARY POWERS'S JOURNAL AND DIARY** Captain Francis Gary Powers's U-2 "spy plane" was 1,300 miles inside the borders of the Soviet Union on a Central Intelligence Agency reconnaissance mission when it was downed by a surface-to-air missile on May 1, 1960. Powers survived the crash by parachuting from the immobilized aircraft, but he was captured on the ground. The international incident escalated Cold War tensions and led to the cancellation of a planned Paris summit between Premier Nikita Khrushchev and President Dwight Eisenhower. Powers was convicted of spying and sentenced to ten years in a Russian prison.

While imprisoned, Powers kept a diary of his daily activities. A cellmate encouraged him to write a secret journal as well. In the journal, he described his escape from the plane crash, his capture, the trial, and his estranged relationship with his wife. It was an emotional roller-coaster ride. While in prison he also wove a wool rug with yarn given to him by the mother of his Latvian cellmate. The diary and journal were hidden in the rug when he carried them out of the Soviet Union.

In the journal Powers recalled the instant when the missile hit his aircraft. "I suddenly felt and heard a dull explosion. It was not a bang or a loud noise, but sounded like a 'WHUMP.'"

While drifting by parachute over unknown territory, he contemplated using the CIA suicide pin. "Here again I thought of the torture etc. and unknown horrors that awaited me if I were captured. This led to my thinking of the poisoned pin that I had. It was in a silver dollar coin that had been transformed into a good luck charm. . . . I took off one glove, removed the pin and put it loose into my pocket." Clearly, Powers didn't use the pin. Despite his fears, the Soviets treated him well under the circumstances. He recounted their acts of kindness: government officials took him sightseeing in Moscow during his first few days of captivity and even gave him books to read while in prison.

In February 1962, after serving approximately twenty-one months in prison, Powers was exchanged for the convicted Soviet spy Colonel Rudolph Ivanovich Abel. Powers later remarried and conceived a son, but in 1977, at the age of forty-seven, he died in a helicopter crash while piloting a television news helicopter in Los Angeles. Powers was posthumously awarded the Prisoner of War Medal, the Distinguished Flying Cross, and the National Defense Service Medal on the fortieth anniversary of the U-2 incident, May 1, 2000.

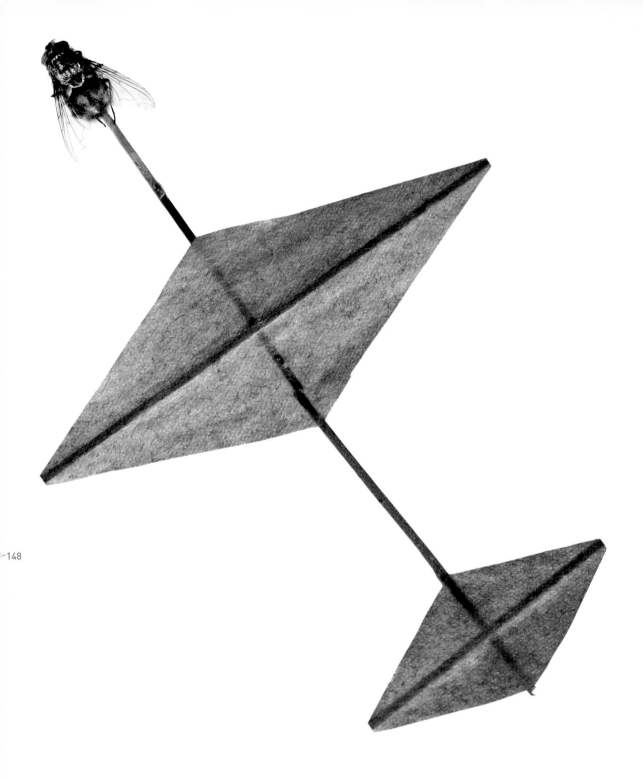

**FLY-POWERED MODEL** Of all the flying machines in the museum, the fly-powered models are the smallest. Made of balsa wood and tissue paper, a single-engine (one-fly) model has a two-inch wingspan, while a twin-engine (two-fly) model has a four-inch wingspan.

Model makers building fly-powered aircraft suggest stretching microfilm (instead of tissue) over one-sixty-fourth-inch strips of balsa for optimum flying performance. A model with a 2½-inch wingspan composed of these materials had a recorded flight time of three minutes when flown indoors by William B. Schwab and Joe Elgin. Flight times on any fly-powered craft will depend on the engine.

Other tips: smaller flies, being lighter than bigger flies, deliver more power for a better climb and glide. Also, the engine is easier to handle when slightly chilled. Placing the fly in a refrigerator freezer for a few seconds will suffice. Experiments suggest that twin-engine models are less efficient than single-engine models. When gluing the engine in place, be careful not to glue the feet. A fly's wings will become stationary if its feet are bound.

Both of these models were built by Frank Ehling and donated to the museum in 1978. The National Air and Space Museum does not endorse the practice of making fly-powered airplanes.

149-

**TRANSMITTER** The Vietnam War saw the introduction of new high-tech weapons to the U.S. arsenal. During the highly classified Operation Igloo White in 1967, sensor devices, incorporating radio transmitters camouflaged as sticks and animal droppings, were placed along the Ho Chi Minh Trail, a myriad of roads, trails, paths, and waterways that was a main enemy supply line. The sensors were used to detect movement and sound along the trail. Their transmissions were interpreted by intelligence analysts using sophisticated computers at a surveillance facility located in Thailand. If the analysts decided that the data indicated enemy troop movements or supply convoys, strike missions by aircraft, usually Phantom F-4 jets, could be launched very quickly.

This transmitter, referred to as Dog Doo, was transferred from the Central Intelligence Agency in 1995. It was intended as a supporting artifact for a future exhibit on the aircraft of the Vietnam War.

**LAZY DOG** The aerial dart is one of the oldest types of air-to-surface weaponry. During World War I, steel darts called flechettes, resembling pointed pencils, were dropped by hand in large quantities at low altitudes from open-cockpit airplanes. Although they were effective against enemy troops and horses, the aircraft were vulnerable to ground fire.

In the early 1950s, the U.S. military developed the Hail missile, later called Lazy Dog, based on the flechette. Shaped like a finned bullet, the new antipersonnel dart was intended to reach ground troops concealed in foxholes and antiaircraft emplacements. Unlike hand-dropped flechettes, Lazy Dog darts were enclosed in cluster bombs (with approximately 11,200 darts per bomb) and dropped from aircraft at high altitudes, out of reach of enemy ground fire.

The Lazy Dog bomb clusters were introduced during the Korean War but were not used in combat by the United States until 1964, in the Vietnam War. It is interesting to note that one of the earliest forms of air-to-surface weaponry was revived and used as late as the Vietnam War.

**ZORI SLIPPERS** When international airlines expanded their routes globally, so did the public's choice of airline. Flight attendants were (and still are) the primary representatives of their companies. In addition to keeping the cabin safe and secure and serving meals and drinks, they also try to give customers individual attention. One airline that prides itself on its in-flight hospitality is Japan Airlines (JAL). As one satisfied JAL traveler put it, "Entering the doorway of a JAL plane is like going through a cultural portal."

These zori slippers, centuries old in design, were worn by kimono-clad JAL cabin attendants on the airline's overseas network from 1954 to 1980.

**GORDON COOPER'S BOOTS** It was just like Gordon Cooper to quit his job and pack his belongings before knowing if he was chosen for the space program. He had returned home from the Lovelace Clinic in New Mexico, where he had undergone excruciating tests as an astronaut candidate, and his confidence in his performance was absolute. On April 9, 1959, NASA announced its selection of seven Mercury astronauts, and Cooper was one of them. On May 15, 1963, he flew MA-9, the final Mercury mission, aboard *Faith 7*.

It's been said, "The new spacesuits were so comfortable that Gordon Cooper, the last man to fly on a Mercury capsule, took a nap during flight." Indeed, he was sporting a newly designed suit, boots, helmet, and gloves, and the mission had a preplanned sleep period — the first for an American space mission. Other first-time space accomplishments included the use of a television camera, but most significant was his ability to control the reentry of his space capsule manually after the automatic controls failed. He splashed down flawlessly in the Pacific Ocean within close range of the recovery ship. Cooper was in space for a total of thirty-four hours, marking the longest flight in the Mercury program.

On August 21, 1965, he made a second orbital flight as commander of Gemini V, with Pete Conrad as pilot. The mission lasted eight days and proved to the world that astronauts could endure spaceflight for the amount of time it took for a trip to the Moon.

Gordon Cooper wore these boots during his Mercury flight.

## WALDO WATERMAN'S AEROBILE

In 1911, aviation pioneer Glenn Curtiss saw a seaplane and said, "Now if we can just take off the wings and drive it down the street." Waldo Waterman of Santa Monica, California, overheard him and took his idea seriously. He put the idea into action twenty-five years later with the development of the first of six "Arrowbile" flying cars in 1936.

The Arrowbile was a combination airplane and automobile. It was powered by a 6-cylinder Studebaker automobile engine that was mounted in the rear of the fuselage and driven by a pusher propeller. The wings could be attached and locked into place from inside the cabin. Automotive manufacturers produced most of the instruments, the tires, and the brakes. The Arrowbile had a top airspeed of 120 miles per hour and ground speed of 70 miles per hour.

The advertising brochure read, "America's New Way to Travel! It's an automobile that flies. Three minutes are required to convert this modern coupe into an airplane. So foolproof, anyone can fly it. Arrowbile has but two controls. One for banking and turning, the other for maintaining a fore and aft

control. It is non-stalling and non-spinning and practically lands itself — can be flown after a short period of instruction. Can be gassed up at neighborhood service stations."

The non-stalling and spinproof aircraft design evolved from Waterman's "Whatsit," a pudgy, tailless, low-winged flivver craft of 1932. The Whatsit had been produced in response to an initiative by the U.S. Bureau of Air Commerce in 1934. The objective was to design an aircraft that was light, easy to fly, and affordable. The target cost was about seven hundred dollars; however, this was found to be impossible to achieve.

Like the Whatsit, the Arrowbile was an aerodynamic success but a financial failure — it proved too expensive to be the "everyman" aircraft of the Great Depression. Waterman, however, kept producing them in small numbers under the name Aerobile. This one was built in the late 1940s with a Tucker automobile engine. It held a certificate of flight worthiness as late as 1957 and carried the registration number N-54P in the experimental category.

## GLENN CURTISS'S MOTORCYCLE

Glenn Curtiss, the man behind the "power" of early aircraft, was born in Hammondsport, New York, in 1878. As a young boy with a passion for speed, he quenched his addiction with hand-built sleds that were the fastest in the neighborhood and ice skates that were powered with sails. In his young adulthood, he opened a cycle shop where he experimented with gas engines and later designed two-cycle motorcycle engines to make his bikes run faster. Initially, he had little interest in aviation, but he saw a market for his engines in the embryonic industry. The Wright brothers weren't interested, but other pilots were keen to have them. His first customer was Thomas Scott Baldwin, who used a Curtiss engine to power his dirigible, the *California Arrow*.

In January 1907, after completing a 40-horsepower, 8-cylinder engine for an airplane, Curtiss wondered how it would perform on the ground. He mounted the engine to a specially built frame and ran it first over the snow-covered ground. Unsatisfied with the results, he crated the motorcycle and shipped it to the warmer conditions of Ormond Beach, Florida. On January 24, with a two-mile head start on the wide sand beach, Curtiss's motorcycle screamed down the seashore at 137 miles per hour. He became the fastest human alive, establishing an unofficial world speed record. The V-8 engine tested from the motorcycle platform became a cornerstone of aircraft-engine design and led to the development of the OX aircraft engines used in World War I.

Curtiss became legendary for his aircraft engines, airplanes, and the first chain of public flying schools that spread across the country. He invented the dual-control trainer; the NC-4 flying boat, which made the first transatlantic flight in 1919; and, with others, the JN-4 "Jenny."

**GREMLIN** The term "gremlin" was made up and used by aviators sometime around World War I. Pilots jokingly blamed all of their aircraft's mechanical failures on gremlins. They were cunning little creatures that sabotaged airplanes. If a plane had an engine failure and made a crash landing, it was the fault of the gremlins. During World War II, the mischievous deeds of these imps were illustrated in U.S. Army Air Forces safety-instruction manuals and films on flying, maintenance, and weather.

In 1943, Royal Air Force pilot Roald Dahl published *The Gremlins*, a children's book telling about the dangers the nasty little beasts posed to RAF pilots and the mis-

haps they caused. The term was already in mainstream popular culture when Walt Disney discovered Dahl's book. He made plans to make a cartoon version of *The Gremlins*, with illustrations more amiable than Dahl's gruesome depictions. The film was canceled, but the company printed a small book and at some point made stuffed replicas of its version of the gremlin, complete with flying goggle and helmet. The Women Airforce Service Pilots (WASPs) even adopted Fifinella, Disney's female gremlin, as its mascot.

This gremlin, produced by the Walt Disney Company, was given to the museum by aviation pioneer Alexander de Seversky.

When I peered into an aged wooden crate and saw Anne Morrow Lindbergh's belongings for the first time, I felt as if I had found a sunken treasure. Her personal items had been stored for decades with her husband's spare equipment from their flights aboard the *Tingmissartoq* and had just been uncovered. Among the flight clothing, food rations, and survival tools, I spotted her radio operator's manual — the one mentioned in *North to the Orient*. Thumbing through it, I discovered a delicate dried flower. It had been picked by her and placed between the pages over seventy years ago. With goose bumps on my arms, it became obvious that *Artifacts of Flight* was taking me on a personal expedition — through the collections of the National Air and Space Museum.

As a staff photographer at the museum, my assignments have covered the icons on public display and the eccentricities tucked away in storage. I thought readers would be interested to know that aside from the airplanes, we also have a stuffed lion named Gilmore, a flying car, and a compilation of motion-sickness containers (known to all as "barf bags") in the collection. My plan for this book was to portray a sample of artifacts with an artistic vision, bring to the fore ones that called for closer attention, and unveil the hidden for all to see.

The selection began with my simple list of favorites. The remaining gaps were filled with suggestions from museum staff and research. I pored through hundreds of original documents in the registrar's office and thousands of digital files on a computer database system listing more than 45,000 artifacts. The candidate objects were then taken off display or pulled from storage (after a trail of requests and with the assistance of curators and technicians) before each photograph was taken.

Once in front of the camera, the artifacts often challenged me. What was I to do with 110 yards of silk from a parachute belonging to Tiny Broadwick, the first woman parachutist? How could I show the size of a miniature message capsule used by pigeons during World War I? Heads turned as I carried a naked female mannequin over my shoulder across the storage complex — to clothe it in Tiny's parachute. And ears pricked when I asked for a pigeon from the Division of Birds at the National Museum of Natural History. The request was immediately honored with a frozen pigeon. With the help of a coworker (because I was too squeamish), the capsule was firmly attached to the poor bird's leg.

Through the camera's lens, the artifacts came to life. Whether in a defined crinkle on a letter written by George Washington or the smooth edge of a scissor blade used to cut Amelia Earhart's hair, I became aware of their individualized qualities. I also learned the human meaning of each artifact. A couple of religious medals carried by astronaut Ed White on his spacewalk symbolized faith. The stopwatch used by Wilbur Wright to time the first powered flights in 1903 was a sign of hope. A stuffed monkey, burlap doll, and magnesium safety pins — all were good-luck charms, representing the fear pilots sometimes felt. I laughed over the absurdity of insect-powered models and was dismayed at the misfortune of the Apollo 1 astronauts depicted on a now sadly ironic safety poster.

Through text and photographs, I have attempted to relay their stories and to portray their pertinence and beauty. It is my hope that these chosen eyewitnesses provide a sense of discovery and a new visual dimension to the amazing history of flight.

# afterword by carolyn russo

Carolyn Russo is a photographer
at the Smithsonian Institution
National Air and Space Museum

**ACKNOWLEDGMENTS** The assistance, support, suggestions, and favors of many individuals are the essential ingredients to any book project. Beginning with my family, I owe my husband, Robert A. Craddock, and son, Maxwell, many thanks (and several dinners) for the times my computer and papers greeted them at the dining-room table instead of food. My husband was my sounding board, initial proofreader, and at times personal editor. I thank my four-year-old son for somehow understanding when my attention was taken away from him with this project.

To the staff at Abrams, especially Eric Himmel and Michael Walsh, thank you. I am truly grateful to Eric Himmel for bringing his own talent to this book as editor-in-chief, to Joseph Cho and Stefanie Lew at Binocular for their design, and to editor Richard Slovak for his attention to detail.

A special thanks to Senator John Glenn for his foreword and to Ted A. Maxwell at the National Air and Space Museum for his introduction and constant support. Thanks for the assistance of Tonya McKirgan at the John Glenn Institute at Ohio State University, and to John R. Dailey, Peter Golkin, Trish Graboske, and Scotty O'Connell at the National Air and Space Museum.

To the rest of the museum staff, I am indebted. Thanks to Dana Bell, Barb Brennan, Claire Brown, Greg Bryant, Paul Ceruzzi, Helen Cheek, Dorothy Cochrane, Martin Collins, Roger Connor, Tom Crouch, Dik Daso, Tom Dietz, Thang Duong, Phil Edwards, Gary Fletcher, Ellen Folkama, Doris Fulton, David Gant, Dittmar Geiger, Dan Hagedorn, Dave Heck, Kate Igoe, Peter Jakab, Pat Jellison, Kristine Kaske, Melissa Keiser, Jeremy Kinney, Russ Lee, Cathy Lewis, Suzanne Lewis, Priscilla Limes, Joanne London, LeRoy London, Don Lopez, Anita Mason, Helen Morrill, Beatrice Mowry, Valerie Neal, Allan Needell, Tommy Nguyen, Brian Nicklas, Dave Paper, Laurenda Patterson, Norine Person, Dom Pisano, Chris Pratt, Natalie Rjedkin-Lee, David Romanowski, Liz Scheffler, Phouy Sengsourinh, Tom Soapes, Alex Spencer, Rose Steinat, Pris Strain, Deborah Swinson, Mark Taylor, Toni Thomas, Tina Tyson, Bob van der Linden, Patti Williams, Frank Winter, and Mandy Young.

Without the assistance of the staff at the Garber Facility (with the responsibility of the movement of objects), this book would not have been possible. Thanks to Tom Alison, Al Bachmeier, Carl Bobrow, Chuck Burton, Doug Dammann, Sam Dargan, John Eckstine, John Fulton, Samantha Gallagher, Ken Isbell, Wilbert Lee, Ed Marshall, Lars McLamore, Bob McLean, Ed McManus, Jeff Mercer, Thomas S. Momiyama, Matt Nazzaro, Scott Neel, Bill Reese, Carolyn Triebel, Jeannie Whited, Charlie William Whittaker, Scott Willey, Dave Wilson, Tom Yarker, and a very special thanks to Lillie Wiggins for her gracious assistance, suggestions, and company.

I am grateful to my dedicated research volunteer Magda Wolff for reading, copying, and organizing files, and to my coworkers and volunteers for their photography assistance, including Mark Avino, Ramsey Gorchev, Eric Long, Amy McColeman, and Chuck Moore.

Thanks to Edie Hedlin and Sarah Stauderman at the Smithsonian Institution Archives, Lorie Aceto, John Dillaber, Hugh Talman, Jeff Tinsley, and Jim Wallace at the Smithsonian Office of Imaging and Photographic Services, John Sokolowski at Integration Technologies Group, Inc., Paul Woofter and Michael Burton at Ilford Imaging USA Inc., Fred Engle at the Chief of Naval Operations Environmental Readiness Division, David B. Des Roches at the Defense Security Cooperation Agency, and Joseph D. Buckley for his information about carrier pigeons at Chatham Naval Air Station in *Wings over Cape Cod*.

To my parents, Joan and John, Kate Russo, and Mary Craddock, thank you. To Anna Fili-Astofone, Eva Fadel, Gene Hemrick, Eva Russo, Aimee Russo, Vincent Russo, and Lissa Stewart, thanks for listening. And finally, thank you, Mother Mary, for answering my prayers.

**LIST OF ARTIFACTS** Page numbers refer to the photographs; accompanying text may be on the facing page.

**PIONEERS AND EARLY FLIGHT**
airmail. *See* Byrd
altitude correction computer, 38
ballooning: letter by George Washington, 128–29; oldest known photograph, 129; posters, 52
Broadwick, Tiny: parachute, 48
Byrd, Richard E.: airmail bag, 30; radio transmitter, 60
Chanute, Octave: anemometer, 66
Curtiss, Glenn: motorcycle, 154–55
Doolittle, Jimmy: flying goggles, 36; Joe (Mrs. James) Doolittle's signature tablecloth, 37
Douglas World Cruiser *Chicago*, 59
Earhart, Amelia: goggles, 47; Lockheed Vega, 46; radio, 61; scissors, 98–99; trophy, 98
early pilot licenses, 22
early plane tickets, 106
Goddard, Robert: A-Series rocket, 114; liquid-fuel rocket engine, 44
*Hindenburg* relics, 18, 19
Lindbergh, Anne Morrow: radio manual and control stick, 64–65
Lindbergh, Charles: Caribbean map, 111; flying suit and helmet, 68, 69; passport photo, 23; *Spirit of St. Louis*, 8, 54, 55, 67
Lowell, Percival: Mars globe, 63
*Norge* (airship): food ration, 138–39
parachute. *See* Broadwick; Popular Culture and Memorabilia: Gilmore
Post, Wiley: map, 27; stratosphere suit, 26
*Spirit of St. Louis. See* Lindbergh
Steiner, John. *See* ballooning: oldest known photograph
Vin Fiz: airplane, 50–51; bottle, 50
Wagstaff, Patty: flight jacket and earrings, 49

Wright brothers: letter by Wilbur Wright, 110; propeller fragment, 144; stopwatch, 14; Wright Flyer, 15. See also Chanute See also Military Aviation: Mitchell

**EXPERIMENTATION**

Bell Rocket Belt, 74
Bertelsen, William: Aeromobile, 112
Flying Pancake (Vought V-173), 75
Gordon, Robert: liquid-fuel engine, 45
human pickup harness, 35
Neu, Ed: liquid-fuel Super P Engine, 45
Northrop, Jack: Flying Wing (N-1M), 120, 121
Princeton Air Rho Car, 113
silent propeller, 109
Waterman, Waldo: Aerobile, 154–55
X-15, 90
Yeager, Charles "Chuck": flight suit, 89
See also Pioneers and Early Flight: Curtiss; Goddard; Wright brothers; Space: Art; RX-1

**MILITARY AVIATION**

aircraft spotter cards, 76
American flag, 28
antipersonnel darts (Lazy Dog), 151
Arnold, Henry H. "Hap": five stars, 108
aviator's face mask (World War I), 126
Blackbird (SR-71 reconnaissance aircraft; details), 2–3, 4–5, 136, 137
carrier pigeon. See message capsule
Cochran, Jackie: WASP handbag and gloves, 81
Cuban Missile Crisis model, 146
Enola Gay: arming plug, 85; bomb-sight, 84
Garber, Paul: target kite, 82. See also Popular Culture and Memorabilia: kite
goggles (World War I), 126–27

Hultgreen, Lt. Kara: flight jacket, 144–45
Humanitarian Daily Rations (HDRs), 139
LeMay, Curtis E.: cigar, 77
message capsule (World War I), 31
Mitchell, Billy: tricycle, 134
Powers, Francis Gary: journal and diary, 146–47
Purnell, Louis R.: Tuskegee Airman's glove with medals, 78–79
transmitter (Dog Doo), 150
Tuskegee Airmen. See Purnell
U-2. See Powers
WASPs. See Cochran

**SPACE**

Able (monkey), 34
Anita (spider), 32
Apollo 11: bumper sticker, 53; stopwatch, 72
Apollo 13: air-filtration device, 96; towing invoice, 97
Apollo-Soyuz mission: Apollo Command Service Module (detail), 142; commemorative cigarettes, 143
Armstrong, Neil: dip form (Apollo program), 73
Art (test dummy), 42, 43
autographed dollar bills (Apollo program), 95
butterflies, 101
Cooper, Gordon: boots (Mercury flight), 153
Fallen Astronaut statuette, 140
Gemini VII: American flag, 118; spacecraft, 119
Glenn, John: applesauce (Mercury flight), 21; camera (Mercury flight), 6
Grissom, Gus: gloves (Mercury flight), 132; safety poster (Apollo program), 133
Lunar Sample Return Container (Apollo 11), 94
Mercury spacesuit (child-sized), 103

RX-1 Experimental Hard Suit (Apollo program), 123
Saturn V rocket (detail; Apollo program), 130–31
Schirra, Wally: harmonica (Gemini VI), 117
Schmitt, Harrison: boots (Apollo 17), 16–17
Scrabble (Skylab), 32–33
Shepard, Alan: spacesuit (Mercury flight), 20
space foods, 70–71. See also Glenn: applesauce
space shuttles: Enterprise, 40–41, 160; solid rocket motor O-ring heater, 141
Stafford, Thomas: string of bells (Gemini VI), 117
Sullivan, Kathryn: gloves, 100
Valsalva device ("helmet nose scratcher"), 127
White, Ed: religious medals (Gemini IV), 99; safety poster (Apollo program), 133

**POPULAR CULTURE AND MEMORABILIA**

Astron Scout model rocket, 115
boomerang, 39
Buck Rogers: toys, 86–87; Wilma Deering mask, 80
E.T. trading cards, 62
Flash Gordon statuette, 56
fly-powered models, 148, 149
Gilmore: flying lion, 24; his parachute, 25
good-luck charms: burlap doll, 135; Maggie (stuffed monkey), 58; magnesium safety pins (from bombs), 29
gremlin, 156
kite, 83. See also Military Aviation: Garber
lunchbox, 122
mothership (Close Encounters of the Third Kind), 92–93
motion-sickness containers, 104–5

opium pipes, 125
poster: 50th anniversary of flight, 102
premium rings (Captain Midnight, Sky King), 57
sheet music, 116
tights (worn by Braniff flight attendants), 124
travelers' insurance machine, 107
USS Enterprise (Star Trek), 41
Zori slippers (worn by Japan Airlines flight attendants), 152
See also Pioneers and Early Flight: Doolittle: Joe Doolittle; Space: autographed dollar bills; Apollo-Soyuz mission: commemorative cigarettes; Mercury spacesuit; Schirra; Stafford